The request, brought by carrier-pigeon to your retreat on Takio in the Isles of the Dawn, is perfectly clear. An experienced adventurer is desperately needed in the distant city of Arion for a mission of deadly importance — an adventurer like YOU. When you arrive at the court of King Jonthane after a long sea voyage, the urgency of the mission becomes clear. Telessa, the beautiful young Princess Royal, is missing, believed kidnapped. She must be rescued, and must be rescued fast.

Unfortunately, in his haste King Jonthane has already given the quest to another, your deadly rival, Fang-zen of Jitar! He cannot be trusted — you know that the only person suitable for this heroic task is YOU. Can you prove that you are the one to rescue the princess — and, more importantly, find her, wherever she may be held, before she can be harmed? Hurry, for time is running out!

Two dice, a pencil and an eraser are all you need to embark on this thrilling adventure, which comes complete with its own elaborate combat system and a score sheet to record your progress. Many dangers lie ahead and your success is anything but certain. It's up to YOU to decide which route to follow, which dangers to risk and which foes to fight. Can you venture into the heart of Deathmoor and return with the princess safe and sound?

Fighting Fantasy Gamebooks

FIGHTING FANTASY – The Introductory Role-Playing Game
THE RIDDLING REAVER – Four Thrilling Adventures

The Fighting Fantasy Novels
THE TROLLTOOTH WARS – Chaos Invades Allansia
DEMONSTEALER – Chadda Darkmane Returns
SHADOWMASTER – Chadda Darkmane and Death

The Advanced Fighting Fantasy System
OUT OF THE PIT – Fighting Fantasy Monsters
TITAN – The Fighting Fantasy World
DUNGEONEER – An Introduction to the World of Role-playing Games
BLACKSAND! – More Advanced Fighting Fantasy

Steve Jackson and Ian Livingstone

present

DEATHMOOR

by Robin Waterfield

Illustrated by Russ Nicholson

PUFFIN BOOKS

PUFFIN BOOKS

Published by the Penguin Group
Penguin Books Ltd, 27 Wrights Lane, London w8 5tz, England
Penguin Books USA Inc., 375 Hudson Street, New York, New York 10014, USA
Penguin Books Australia Ltd, Ringwood, Victoria, Australia
Penguin Books Canada Ltd, 10 Alcorn Avenue, Toronto, Ontario, Canada m4v 3b2
Penguin Books (NZ) Ltd, 182–190 Wairau Road, Auckland 10, New Zealand

Penguin Books Ltd, Registered Offices: Harmondsworth, Middlesex, England

First published 1994
1 3 5 7 9 10 8 6 4 2

Typeset by Datix International Ltd, Bungay, Suffolk
Filmset in Monophoto Palatino
Printed in England by Clays Ltd, St Ives plc

CONTENTS

For Kathy, for fun

INTRODUCTION

You are an adventurer: an experienced, battle-hardened warrior. A native of the seaport Chalannabrad, in the Old World, you are as familiar with the ways of the sea as with those of the land. In fact, you were resting on Takio, the northernmost of the Isles of Dawn, diving for scarlet pearls among the reefs and shoals (and sharks) when word reached you of a gathering of adventurers like yourself in the city of Arion in distant Khul.

Some great quest is clearly under way. But before you can travel to Arion and offer your services, you must find out whether your holiday has fully restored your powers. You will use dice to find out your initial SKILL, STAMINA and LUCK scores. On pp. 16–17 there is an *Adventure Sheet* which you may use to record details of your adventure: enter your SKILL, STAMINA and LUCK scores there. You are advised either to use a pencil for writing on the *Adventure Sheet*, or to make photocopies of the page to use in future adventures.

Skill, Stamina and Luck

Roll one dice. Add 6 to this number and enter this total in the SKILL box on the *Adventure Sheet*.

Roll two dice. Add 12 to the number rolled, then enter this total in the STAMINA box.

There is also a LUCK box. Roll one dice, add 6 to this number and enter the total in the LUCK box.

For reasons that will be explained below, SKILL, STAMINA and LUCK scores change constantly during any adventure. You must keep an accurate record of these scores, and for this reason you are advised either to write small in the boxes or to keep an eraser handy. But never rub out your *Initial* scores. Although you may be awarded additional SKILL, STAMINA and LUCK points, these totals may never exceed your *Initial* scores, unless you are specifically told otherwise.

Your SKILL score is a measure of your expertise with weapons and in other situations requiring skills: the higher the better. Your STAMINA score reflects your physical condition – the higher your STAMINA score, the longer you will be able to survive in your adventure. Your LUCK score indicates how naturally lucky a person you are. May your gods smile on you and grant you a generous LUCK score!

Battles

You will often come across entries where you are told to fight a creature of some sort. An option to flee may be given, but if not — or if you choose to attack the creature anyway — you must resolve the battle as follows.

First record the creature's SKILL and STAMINA scores in the first empty Encounter Box on your *Adventure Sheet*. The scores for each creature are given in the book every time you have an encounter.

The sequence of combat is then:

1. Roll two dice once for your opponent. Add its SKILL score. This total is the creature's Attack Strength.

2. Roll two dice once for yourself. Add the number rolled to your current SKILL score. This total is your Attack Strength.

3. If your Attack Strength is higher than that of your opponent you have wounded it; proceed to step 4. If your opponent's Attack Strength is higher than yours, it has wounded you; proceed to step 5. If both Attack Strengths are the same, you have avoided each other's blows — start the next Attack Round from step 1, above.

4. You have wounded the creature, so subtract 2 points from its STAMINA score. You may use your LUCK here to do additional damage (see below).

5. The creature has wounded you, so subtract 2 points from your own STAMINA score. You may use LUCK here to lessen the damage you have taken (see below).

6. Make the appropriate adjustments to either your opponent's or your own STAMINA score (and your LUCK score if you used LUCK).

7. Begin the next Attack Round by repeating steps 1–6. This sequence continues until the STAMINA score of either yourself or the creature you are fighting has been reduced to zero, which is death.

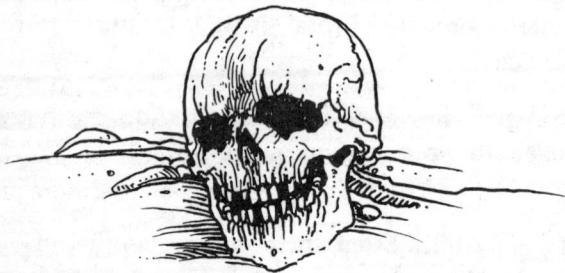

Fighting More Than One Creature

If you come across more than one creature in a particular encounter, the instructions on that page will tell you how to handle the battle. Sometimes you will treat the group as a single opponent; sometimes you will fight each one in turn.

Luck

At various times during your adventure, either in battles or when you are faced with situations in which you could be either lucky or unlucky (details of these are given in the relevant paragraphs), you may call on your LUCK to make the outcome more favourable. But beware! Using LUCK is a risky business and, if you are unlucky, the results could be disastrous.

The procedure for using your LUCK is as follows. Roll two dice. If the number rolled is equal to or less than your current LUCK score, you have been Lucky and the result will go in your favour. If the number rolled is higher than your current LUCK score, you have been Unlucky and you will be penalized.

This procedure is known as *Testing your Luck*. Each time you *Test your Luck*, you must subtract 1 point from your current LUCK score, regardless of the outcome. Thus you will soon realize that the more you rely on luck, the more risky this will become.

Using Luck in Battles

In certain paragraphs you will be instructed to *Test your Luck* and will then be told the consequences of being Lucky or Unlucky. However, in battles, you always have the option of using your LUCK, either to inflict more serious damage on a creature you have just wounded or to minimize the effects of being wounded yourself.

If you have just wounded your opponent, you may *Test your Luck* as described above. If you are Lucky, you have inflicted a severe wound and may subtract 2 *extra* points from the creature's STAMINA score. However, if you are Unlucky, the wound turns out to be a mere graze and you must restore 1 point to the creature's STAMINA (so that, instead of scoring the normal 2 points of damage, you now score only 1).

If your opponent has just wounded you, you may *Test your Luck* to try to minimize the wound. If you are Lucky, you have managed to avoid the full damage of the blow; restore 1 point of STAMINA (so that, instead of causing 2 points of damage, it causes only 1). If you are Unlucky, you have taken a more serious blow and must subtract 1 *extra* STAMINA point from your total.

Remember that, whatever happens, you must subtract 1 point from your LUCK score each time you *Test your Luck*.

Restoring Skill, Stamina and Luck

Skill

Your SKILL score will not change much during your adventure. Occasionally you may be told to decrease your SKILL score (as the result of a serious wound to your fighting arm, say) or to increase it (as a result of finding a magical weapon, for instance). Your SKILL score cannot exceed its *Initial* value unless you are specifically told that it can. Drinking the Potion of Skill (see below) will restore your SKILL to its *Initial* level at any time except in the middle of a battle.

Stamina and Provisions

Your STAMINA score will change a lot during your adventure as you fight and undertake arduous tasks. As you near your goal, your STAMINA level may be dangerously low and battles may be particularly risky, so be careful!

Your pouch and water flask contain enough Provisions for ten meals. You may rest and eat at any time except when engaged in a battle. Eating a meal restores 4 STAMINA points. When you eat a meal, add 4 points to your STAMINA score and deduct 1 point from your Provisions. A separate Provisions Remaining box is provided on the *Adventure Sheet* for recording details of your Provisions. Remember that you have a long way to go, so use your Provisions wisely!

Remember too that your STAMINA score may never exceed its *Initial* value unless you are specifically told that it can. Drinking the Potion of Strength (see below) will restore your STAMINA to its *Initial* level at any time except in the middle of a battle.

Luck

Additions to your LUCK score may be awarded during the adventure when you have been particularly lucky. Details are given in the appropriate paragraphs of the book. The main way in which your LUCK score will decrease is through *Testing your Luck*. As with SKILL and STAMINA, your LUCK score may never exceed its *Initial* value unless you are told that it can. Drinking the Potion of Fortune (see below) will restore your LUCK to its *Initial* level *and* will increase your *Initial* LUCK by 1 point.

Equipment and Potions

You will start your adventure with a bare minimum of equipment, but you may stumble across other items during your travels. You are armed with a sword and are dressed in leather armour. You have a pouch to hold some of your Provisions and money, and a backpack to hold anything else you may wish to keep. In addition to ten meals' worth of Provisions, you start your adventure with 20 Gold Pieces (and 1 scarlet pearl). Make a note of these items on your *Adventure Sheet*.

In addition, you may take *one* bottle of a magical potion which will aid you on your quest. You may choose to take a bottle of any of the following:

Potion of Skill – restores SKILL points
Potion of Strength – restores STAMINA points
Potion of Fortune – restores LUCK points and adds 1
 to *Initial* LUCK

This potion may be taken at any time during your adventure (except when engaged in a battle). Taking a potion will restore SKILL, STAMINA or LUCK points to their *Initial* level (the Potion of Fortune will also add 1 point to your *Initial* LUCK score before your LUCK is restored). Make a note on your *Adventure Sheet* when you have drunk a potion.

ADVENTURE SHEET

SKILL *Initial* *Skill=*	STAMINA *Initial* *Stamina=*	LUCK *Initial* *Luck=*

EQUIPMENT:

GOLD:

POTIONS:

NOTES:

PROVISIONS REMAINING:

MONSTER ENCOUNTER BOXES

Skill=	*Skill=*	*Skill=*
Stamina=	*Stamina=*	*Stamina=*

Skill=	*Skill=*	*Skill=*
Stamina=	*Stamina=*	*Stamina=*

Skill=	*Skill=*	*Skill=*
Stamina=	*Stamina=*	*Stamina=*

Skill=	*Skill=*	*Skill=*
Stamina=	*Stamina=*	*Stamina=*

BACKGROUND

The western stretches of the Black Ocean are notorious for sudden squalls and storms. You pray to Hydana, god of waters, and beseech him to distract his brother Sukh the storm-god – or at least to divert him to some other part of the world. Perhaps Hydana hears you, but Sukh is a mighty god, capable of manifesting his power in many places at once. At any rate, the Black Ocean lives up to its reputation . . .

It takes you five days and nights to battle in your solo craft through the storm. At last, as the sun sinks in fire under the ocean, in the distance you glimpse the looming cliffs of the Rockwall Islands in the south-west. Only two more days, then, to Arion, if the weather holds.

At noon on the third day you find a space in the crowded quays of Arion and make your way up the hill towards the royal palace. The city is as busy as usual, with people going about their daily business, but there is a curious listlessness about their actions. Your fame may gain you entry to the king and queen themselves; if not, the Noble Council of Elders will tell you what is going on and the reason for the summoning of adventurers to Arion.

King Jonthane and his sister Elegana, the co-rulers of Arion, are indeed only too glad to hear of your arrival, and you do not have to wait long before you are summoned to the royal presence.

'If only you'd arrived yesterday,' Queen Elegana exclaims, as soon as you are standing before them. 'Or, better, if only you'd never left after your last visit here – when was it? Three years ago?'

'Closer to four, my lady,' you reply, and you shudder at the memory of the evil you encountered then. 'But what can I do for you now?'

'Nothing,' the king replies bluntly. 'I had to award the quest to another. Time is vital, you see. You weren't here, so I gave it to . . .' He gulps before continuing. '. . . Fang-zen of Jitar!' The king holds up his hand to forestall your protests. 'I know, I know, he's a nasty piece of work. But even you have to admit that he's pretty good at what he does. And I had to choose the best available. It's my daughter, you see.'

Over the next ten minutes, the king stammers out his tale. His daughter, the Princess Royal Telessa — only fifteen years of age, but already famed throughout Khul for her beauty and charm — had been kidnapped a few weeks before, while out riding with some friends just north of the city. The kidnappers showed they meant business. The limbs of her friends had been hacked from their bodies and left on the ground in the form of a message: WAIT.

Jonthane and Elegana of Arion are no fools, however. While seeming to await the kidnappers' message, they secretly sent out carrier-pigeons in all directions. One of them found you on Takio. If it weren't for the storm, you'd have been here on time.

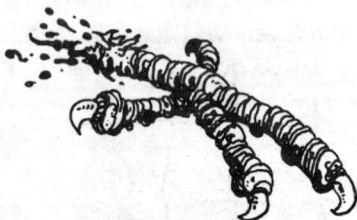

'No message arrived until two days ago,' Jonthane continues. 'I was so anxious ... my precious, my Telessa ... When it came, it was no simple demand. They — whoever they are, for the message was un-signed — they want total control, for ever, over the export of gold from the rich mines which Arion controls. Now, this is far from being our only export, but it is certainly a rich source of revenue. I have to send a letter of agreement to the demand, signed with

20

the royal seal, in the hands of a single messenger. The messenger is to travel due west of the city, alone, until the kidnappers meet him.'

'How will the kidnappers make themselves known to the messenger?' you ask.

'Their message was accompanied by locks of Telessa's hair, crudely shorn with some blunt knife. Her hair is unmistakable, like fine-spun gold, shot through with russet light. They will greet the messenger with more of her hair – or with her head if the messenger fails to bring my letter, or does not travel alone.'

You stay with the king and queen for some minutes more, offering to help in any way you can. But it is too late: your rival, Fang-zen, has the job. 'What did you offer him?' you ask. 'The usual fee for such work,' the king replies. 'Half our kingdom.'

When it is appropriate to do so, you leave the royal presence and wander back into town. Turn to **1**.

1

Several hours and several taverns later, you find your-self in the dockland area of the city, in a seedy dive called 'The Barnacled Keel'. Talking of barnacled keels, the warts on the barman's face ... It seems that, however much you drink, the clearer your head becomes. The image of the beautiful young princess being manhandled by ruffians keeps appearing in your mind, and makes you curse your bad luck in failing to reach Arion in time. Will you travel west out of Arion anyway, to see if you can find Fang-zen or the kidnappers (turn to **200**), or will you stay in Arion (turn to **64**)?

2

Two giant rats scuttle out of a hole in the passage wall and attack you. You will have to fight them separately. Fight one of them — whichever one you choose — as normal. The other rat gets a free attack against you: if its Attack Strength is higher than yours in any Attack Round, it injures you, but you cannot wound it because you are occupied in fighting its cousin.

	SKILL	STAMINA
First GIANT RAT	5	4
Second GIANT RAT	5	4

If you win and you want to put your hand into the hole the rodents came out of in order to see what you can find, turn to **40**. Otherwise, continue down the tunnel by turning to **275**.

3

You succeed only in disturbing a family of large rats, one of which nips you on the forearm. Reduce your STAMINA by 1 point, then leave the room by turning to **80**.

4

You have scarcely entered the margins of a marsh when the mists come down. You try to retreat out of the marsh but, whichever way you turn, you seem to be going deeper into it. You sit, shivering, for hours on a grassy tussock but it looks as though the mist will never clear. You hope that you can catch a glimpse of the sun to restore your sense of direction as well as your hope, but the mists are too thick, and eventually you're no longer sure whether it is daytime or moonlit night. Will you sit and wait a little longer (turn to **212**) or get up, even though any movement seems hopeless (turn to **236**)?

5

'Ha! I might have guessed *you*'d turn up,' Fang-zen sneers. 'And you want to fight me? You must be joking. You aren't worth it.' He turns his back on you and pretends to be deeply interested in what one of the other men is saying. Will you strike him while his back is turned (turn to **390**) or turn and leave the bar (turn to **87**)?

6

You turn to a nearby hut, but a black-feathered arrow wings towards you from an unseen archer. It just grazes you (lose 1 STAMINA point), but it puts you off searching the village. You can continue to the north (turn to **207**) or turn west (turn to **34**).

7

Ogres are not noted for their intelligence. 'Me?' he says. 'There's no one living here called Me.' He pulls a double-headed axe from his belt and lumbers down the pathway. You just have time to get to your feet and draw your sword. Turn to **397**.

8

The mist descends again, but you are walking up a slope, so you carry on, hoping that at the top you will break through into sunshine. Anyway, if you carry on climbing, in as straight as line as possible, you can't go wrong, can you? The slope isn't particularly steep, but a terrible weariness overcomes you and you feel as though you want to sleep. *Test your Luck*. If you are Lucky, turn to **295**; if you are Unlucky, turn to **81**.

9

The floor is clearly visible now, some way below you, but there is one more side tunnel for you to float past (turn to **67**) or enter (turn to **33**).

10

You step out along the cobbled street until you catch up with the ghastly hag. 'Here,' you say, 'I'll buy some of your heather. How much is it?' You find her price of 1 Gold Piece outrageous, but she insists that the heather is *really* lucky. Will you pay her price (turn to **83**) or not (turn to **388**)?

11

The roof bursts into flame with a satisfying roar, and soon the elders are pouring out of the hut, coughing and half blinded by the smoke. You laugh silently to yourself from your vantage point behind one of the other huts. You are about to leave the village when you see one of the elders hesitate then dash back into the smoke-filled hut! Will you follow him (turn to 120) or make your escape while the village is in chaos (turn to 302)?

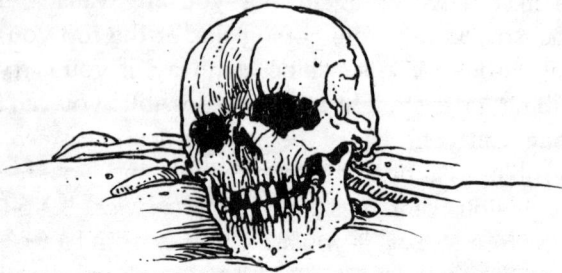

12

You step forward and discover the huddled figure of a middle-aged peasant woman: she is dying from a terrible beating. Before breathing her last, however, she manages to gasp out her tale. The half-giant, Otus, forced her to put him up in her cottage. She was the only one in the village he feared at all, since she was a medicine woman and knew a few potions and spells, and he wanted to keep an eye on her while he waited for you to arrive from Arion. Late last night she tried to burn him alive by setting fire to her own home and then fleeing, but he followed her, unharmed, and caught up with her in a stand of oak trees. Once he had finished with her, he left her for dead. 'But I wasn't quite dead,' she says. 'I came home to die. And he dropped something while he was busy murdering me. I don't know what it is, but I've put an Invisibility spell on it.' She tells you how to undo the spell, then slips gently into death. When you find yourself in a stand of oaks, add 50 to the number of the paragraph you are at, and you will find whatever it is Otus lost. For now, you bury the woman with reverence and leave the village. You feel too sad to spend the night with her ghost in what remains of her cottage, so you camp out in the open. Turn to **278**.

13

The vile flames die down again and the smoke parts to form a kind of archway. You tentatively walk through . . . and there, spread out before you, are the ruins of the central temple of the ancient civilization which used to occupy this land. The shattered stones and marble pillars lie in rubble on the ground, no more than knee-high. Nevertheless, there is a powerful aura of goodness in this place, and that must be why the evil that now inhabits the land set up the miasma to guard it. You are blessed: you may add 2 to your *Initial* LUCK score, and restore your LUCK up to this new level. A sheer cliff rises beyond the ruins; there is no path further north, so you leave the sacred spot and head south. You can now either try to cross the river by means of the bobbing platforms (turn to **269**) or continue southwards past them (turn to **220**).

14

There is deep water on either side of the ford, and in places the shallows are clogged with the river's foul debris, but the ford is still broad enough for you to walk confidently along it. It is also broad enough, however, to offer a secure footing for the Granochin which lives in the river beside it. The monster rises out of the depths, dripping slime and weed, and its talons reach on sinewy arms for your throat.

GRANOCHIN   SKILL 8   STAMINA 10

If you have a throwing-knife, you can use it before you fight to reduce the creature's STAMINA by 4 points *or* its SKILL by 1 point (your choice). If you win, you will not be able to retrieve the knife, however, since the body of the beast will sink back into the depths. If you win, you make it safely the rest of the way to the western bank. Turn to **159**.

15

You made it! You crawl along the passage beyond the lava pool while your ears strain in dread of hearing another fireball approaching behind you. Luckily, nothing happens and you eventually break through the far end of the tunnel. You stand and greedily gulp in great lungfuls of air. Even the bitter air of Deathmoor tastes sweet after your ordeal. You press on with your quest. Turn to **382**.

16

When there is no certainty about which way you should turn, how do you decide? Some crows are wheeling in the air in the distance to the east, so you head in that direction because at least *something* is happening there. It turns out that the crows are circling in anticipation of a feast — a feast of human flesh, which is the kind Khulian crows prefer. Standing at the rise of a low hill, you look down on a man slumped against a solitary, lightning-blasted tree. He is terribly wounded but is still just alive. Where are his assailants? This could be a trap. Will you look for his attackers (turn to **193**) or go down straight away to see if you can help (turn to **344**)?

17

The guard checks, but no one knows of anyone with that name, and there's no one resembling your vague description in the bar where you send the guards. You decide to turn in for the night; turn to **388**.

18

As you make your way down the tunnel it gets smaller and smaller, until you are wriggling along on your stomach, with your sword probing the blackness ahead. You are beginning to wonder if this tunnel will be your tomb. It becomes impossible to keep your backpack on your back. Will you loop it round your belt and trail it behind you (turn to **377**) or push it ahead of you, along with your sword (turn to **175**)?

19

Not all giants are stupid. Otus recognizes you and signals to Ophis. You turn to flee, but a crossbow bolt pierces your heart. Your adventure ends here.

20

You blunder around in the dark, knocking over piles of boxes which turn out to be the Baron's files containing paperwork that goes back for years. The closed room fortunately contains the noise you're making, but you are soon enveloped in an invisible snowstorm of papers. You grab a handful at random and feel around the walls until you find a door. Roll one dice. If you roll a 6, turn to **261**; otherwise, turn to **142**.

21

Roll two dice. If the total is less than, or equal to, your current SKILL score, turn to **186**; otherwise, turn to **118**.

22

You are overcome by fumes before you reach the other side. You lose consciousness and are not aware that your body is falling into the pool of molten lava.

23

As you reach the bar, the landlord is bidding farewell to the man he'd been talking to. All you hear him say is the end of the man's name: '. . . garl, see you then.' He turns to you and demands 1 Gold Piece for the knife-marks you made on his table-top. Will you pay (turn to **48**) or point out that the rest of his furniture is hardly less scarred and battered (turn to **145**)?

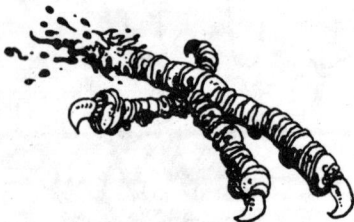

24

You pause after your ordeal and take out your compass to decide where to go next. A slight noise behind you makes you whirl around, and you face a beast you recognize as a Hargon. This bear-like creature always hunts near water, since it lives mainly on fish. But it is not averse to eating warm-blooded creatures. It rears up on its hind legs, its snout wrinkling as its mouth opens in an ear-splitting roar.

HARGON   SKILL 7   STAMINA 10

To your dismay, your compass is irretrievably lost during this fight. If you win, turn to **311**.

25

The rocky faces on either side of you are pitted with natural depressions, some only big enough for a bird to nest in, others almost cave-like. There are also fissures in the ground, none of which are too wide for you to step over. The gulley is narrow and, at this time of day, almost dark, but as you step over one fissure you catch the glint of something white in it. Will you stop to investigate (turn to **121**) or carry on (turn to **146**)?

26

When a small fireball hurtles down the tunnel towards your face, you are able to manoeuvre the shield into position and protect yourself. Turn to **199**.

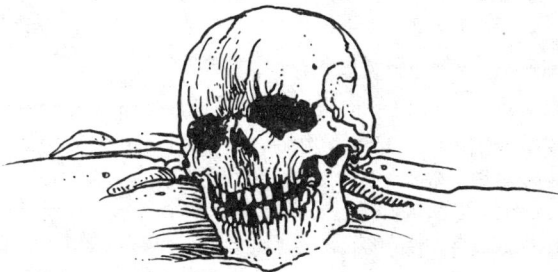

27

The man is dead when you reach him and can tell you nothing now. Night is beginning to fall. You have come from the west, so will you now head north (turn to **289**), south (turn to **57**) or east (turn to **246**)?

28

The huge, gaudy gambling wheel stands upright against a wall at the back of the tavern. If you pay her a Gold Piece, the innkeeper's beautiful assistant will spin the wheel for you. If the wheel stops at the number you bet on, you win double your stake; if not, you lose. Tonight your luck is in. Roll one dice. This is the number of Gold Pieces you win at the Wheel of Fortune. If you won 5 or 6 Gold Pieces, turn to **329**; otherwise, turn to **388**.

29

In order to get back safely, you have to repeat the process of leaping from tussock to tussock that got you here. You can count either from 1 up to 6 or down from 6 to 1 if you prefer. If you ever fall in, turn to **226**. If you are successful all six times, you now turn towards the north, deciding that you should have done this in the first place. Turn to **207**.

30

Regain 1 LUCK point for surviving a difficult fight. Moreover, you find 4 Gold Pieces on Fang-zen's body, together with 3 portions of Provisions and a lamp. But all this is small compensation for the fact that, by the time you try to pick up Otus' trail again, it has gone cold. It is as if he has vanished into thin air. It is now evening, so you decide to rest for the night. There is a village called Outpost a short way to the north, and the edge of a great forest lies to the south. Will you seek shelter in Outpost (turn to **52**) or in the forest (turn to **165**), or will you stay out in the open (turn to **278**)?

31

Will you approach the elders' hut (turn to **360**) or one of the other huts (turn to **198**)?

32

You find only 1 Gold Piece on the Ogre's body and his axe is too heavy for you to wield. Will you now scramble through the open window (turn to **77** or push through the hatch (turn to **237**)?

33

No sooner have you entered the side tunnel than two things happen simultaneously: you see that it is a dead end — and bars clang down over the entrance behind you! If you have some sallow-seed oil, turn to **123**; otherwise, turn to **258**.

34

Before long you reach a place where the tussocks of mud and grass grow sparser and there is more water in between. Will you carry on into this region (turn to **221**) or go north (turn to **207**)?

35

These are poor fishermen and they have never heard of Fang-zen. You can go to the market-place now, if you still need to (turn to **150**), or you can head west out of Arion in search of the kidnappers (turn to **200**).

36

This is the right move. You offer your sword, held flat in both hands, to the nearest skeleton. The dreadful crowd pressing in on you from all sides halts its creaking advance; they can see you are a servant of Good, not of the Evil that reduced them to their present pitiful state. Regain 1 LUCK point. You decide to retrace your steps southwards; turn to **355**.

37

You had the good sense to secrete the implement up your sleeve and now you slip it down into the palm of your hand and set to work on the ropes tying your wrists to the pole. There are two strands of rope to get through. Roll one dice twice. If either roll is a 1 or a 6, turn to **101**; otherwise, turn to **256**.

38

No sooner do your hands touch the window-ledge than a sharp stinging sensation runs down your arms: the Baron's poison is a very effective antidote against would-be burglars. Now you understand how the birds came to die! You scramble quickly back down the ivy. Roll one dice. If the number rolled is even, your body took in enough of the poison to kill you and your adventure ends here! If it is odd, you lose 4 STAMINA points. If you are still alive, you decide to try to lift the hatch which you hope will lead to a cellar. Turn to **242**.

39

Some faint stench of Arachnos' evil invades your spirit. Lose 1 LUCK point then turn back to **253** to try again.

40

A brood of sharp-toothed, baby Giant Rats attach themselves to your fingers and hand. You yelp in pain and surprise, pull your hand out of the hole and shake the creatures off your hand on to the floor, where they wriggle helplessly. Only a sense of urgency stops you taking the time to squash them under your heel. Deduct 2 points from your STAMINA and turn to **275**.

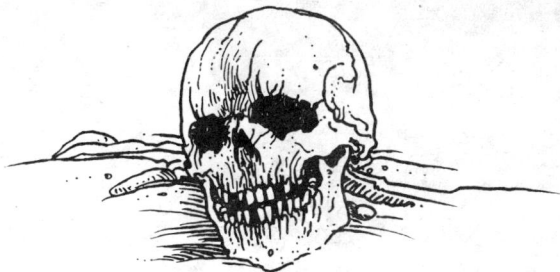

41

The search-party sees you flitting from one hut to another and they release the Rottwild which has been tracking you. The huge hound races towards you and leaps for your throat, its fangs bared in a snarl.

ROTTWILD   SKILL 6   STAMINA 6

If you win, you emerge from the fight to find yourself completely surrounded by Flintskins. Your blood is up now, though: will you try to fight your way free (turn to **166**) or will you surrender (turn to **352**)?

42

You press on towards the south, wondering whether you may have made a mistake. By mid-afternoon you reach an enormous landslip, and now you find yourself at the top of an unscalable cliff. You can hear a waterfall off to your left — that must be yesterday's river. The view is wonderful, but you are not here to be a sightseer, so you turn west along the edge of the cliff. The unusual terrain is home to many rare plants — and to some not-so-common creatures too. Out of nowhere, you are suddenly attacked by a huge Pterolin whose nest is perched on the cliff-face. Its feathers are as black as night, glowing with a brilliant blue sheen in the sunlight; its talons are dripping gore from a recent kill, but it is always hungry for more.

PTEROLIN   SKILL 6   STAMINA 7

If you win, and you have a rope, you can let yourself down to its nest, if you wish (turn to **285**). Otherwise, you continue westwards (turn to **368**).

43

You have been forced to retreat under one of the stilted houses where a ladder leads up to a hole in the middle of the floor of the house. You could either try to climb up the ladder (turn to **149**) or smash through one of the stilts that support the house (turn to **334**); alternatively, you could return to **361** and continue the fight.

44

Your invisible opponent grabs you by the ankles, pulls

you down to the ground and tries to finish you off with a single blow to the head. But as soon as you hit the floor, you roll to one side prior to getting to your feet. Do you roll to the left (turn to 314) or the right (turn to 240)?

45

You stumble in shock and pain, and fall into the river. While you are struggling back up the bank, choking on the foul water, your opponent has no difficulty in finishing you off. Your corpse will join those of the fish in the putrid river.

46

The Flintskins don't know what to make of you. They are not servants of Evil and they sense that you aren't either, but your behaviour has not endeared you to them. They give you back all your possessions and escort you out of their safe gorge, making copious gestures to indicate that they don't want to see you back here again. Turn to 16.

47

You approach the Mere-folk but, since you lack the wherewithal to communicate with them, they interpret your approach as hostile, and they prepare to defend themselves. You cannot kill or wound these insubstantial beings, but if you are successful often enough you will have frightened them off. They wield thin stalks of bulrush, magically empowered so that the lightest touch will injure you in the usual way.

MERE-FOLK   SKILL 6   STAMINA 0

It will take a total of seven successful Attack Rounds, or three in succession, to scare them off. Then turn to **253**.

48

Deduct 1 Gold Piece from your *Adventure Sheet*. You now leave the tavern; turn to **384**.

49

You manage to pull yourself up on to the step. You feel unsafe here, so you clamber up to the landing at the top of the stairs. You can go no higher in the building, and you find that only one of the rooms is safe to enter. But there you make an interesting discovery: the collapse of the staircase has opened up a long-forgotten hiding-place in the wall of the room. Inside is a bottle of potion and a sheet of papyrus, preserved for all these years in their airtight compartment. There is ancient Kabeshian writing on the papyrus, which tells you that the potion is a Potion of Invisibility. Add 1 LUCK point. Now, how will you get down from here? You can jump down from the stairway on to what is left of the ground floor (turn to **115**) or you can jump through the hole in the ground floor into the flooded basement, and pray that the water is deep enough (turn to **157**). If you have a rope, you can find a secure place to tie it and let yourself down safely to the floor. You can then leave the building, but you will also have to leave your rope behind (turn to **219**).

50

On the western side, the Baron's house runs very close to the wall for some distance; to the south, the garden may give you cover once you're in the grounds. Will you climb the western wall (turn to **185**) or the southern wall (turn to **60**)?

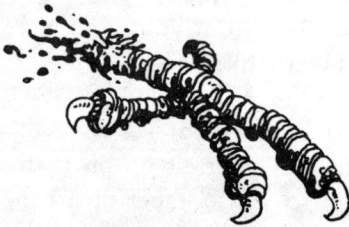

51

You have luckily chosen a spot where, if you can defeat a Wraith quickly enough, you will be able to make a dash for safety.

WRAITH   SKILL 7   STAMINA 8

If you defeat your adversary without taking any hits yourself, turn to **196**; otherwise, turn to **108**.

52

The inhabitants of Outpost lock up early and are deeply suspicious of strangers. Shutters are closed with a bang as you walk down the only street. You get the message: we don't want your kind here. Will you turn around and retrace your steps, or persist in trying to spend the night here? If you stay, turn to **102**. If you leave, the forest is too far away to reach before nightfall, so you must spend the night in the open (turn to **278**).

53

As everyone knows, once the hands of a Ghoul have struck you four times, you are paralysed. But you are still aware. You watch in helpless horror as the Ghoul's yellow teeth draw closer and closer . . .

54

You run away, leaving the Millipede behind, but it continues to follow you. Back at the main tunnel, you turn left and hurry on past the other entrance to the Millipede's lair. Turn to **275**.

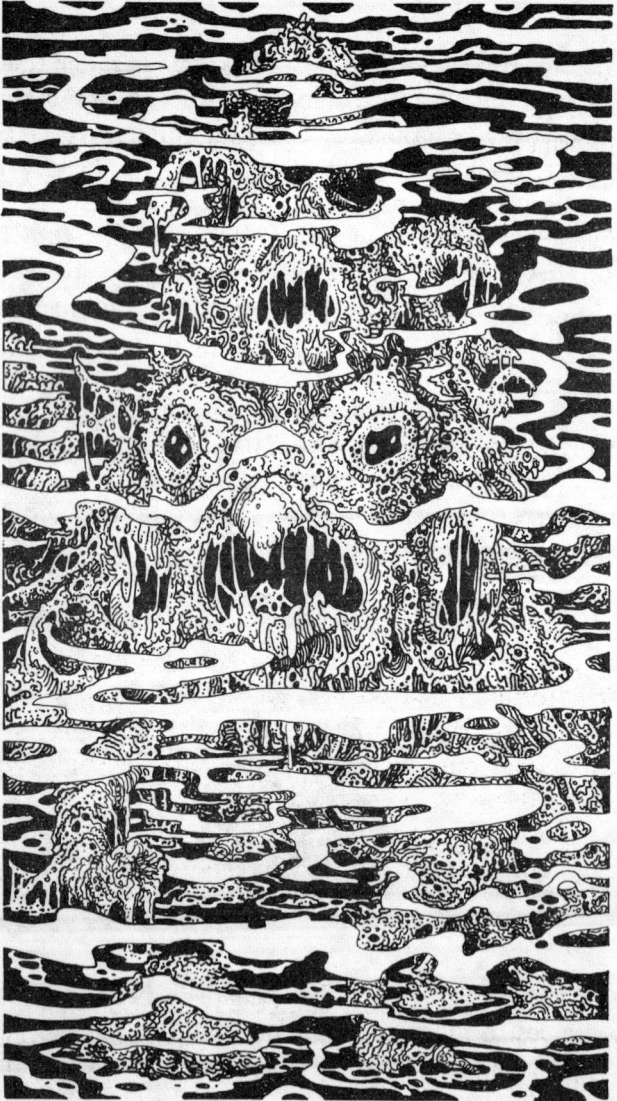

55

After some hours of lonely travel, you are surprised by a vile Slime Monster, an almost shapeless blob of foul-smelling flesh which fights by shooting acid out of its mouths.

SLIME MONSTER   SKILL 9   STAMINA 12

You can escape at any time by turning to either 154 or 214, but in escaping you will have to suffer the loss of 3 STAMINA points. If you win, the vile creature explodes as your sword delivers the killing blow. Roll one dice: if you roll an odd number, you must lose 2 STAMINA points as you are hit by pieces of its acidic flesh. Then turn to 154 or to 214.

56

You present yourself at the guardsman's office. 'Good work,' he says. 'Good observation. Your one-eyed chappie broke down (with a little help from our resident torturer) and confessed. Any time you want a job, just come and talk to me. In the meantime, you can choose one of these three rewards: a Truthstone, 25 Gold Pieces, or a shield. Which do you want?' If you decide on the truthstone, turn to 95; if you go for the money, turn to 357; if you choose the shield, turn to 381.

57

You stumble on as best you can, as night falls and the mists come down, but you are totally confused now. Half-seen, half-recognized shapes loom, eerily glowing, out of the darkness and lure you to your death over a cliff.

58

After a while, the river begins to curve to the west, but the path continues more or less due south. Although it is overgrown with weeds and shrubs, there are occasional patches where you can still see cobblestones: this must once have been a road, long ago. At one point you find a shattered milestone. All you can read of the first line is the first letter, which is 'P', then after some space 'OUS', while the second line reads clearly 'WELL'. Precious Well? Poisonous Well? It's impossible to tell. You carry on, but the road ends abruptly at a huge landslide, which leaves you perched on the top of a huge cliff. There is no further way forward here, and you can hear the sound of a waterfall roaring some way off to your right, as you gaze out over that vast region of Khul known as the Battlegrounds. You decide that your safest option will be to return to the ford you passed earlier; turn to **14**.

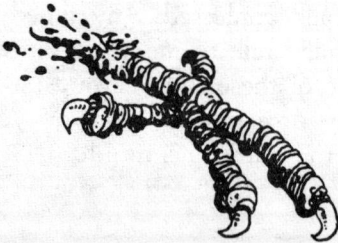

59

There is only one way to go along the passage which ends at a T-junction, where you can turn left or right. The tunnel to the right looks dusty and unused and is only dimly lit; the one to the left is lit by many torches and you can hear indistinct sounds of activity coming from it. Will you turn right (turn to **131**) or left (turn to **272**)?

60

You scramble up the wall, assisted by a low-hanging branch of a rare Allansian Flare tree, part of the Baron's renowned arboretum. You rest on top of the wall and peer around. Beyond the flower-bed a well-kept lawn stretches almost to the rear of the house. A number of unusual trees stand in the grounds, and there are also patches of dense shrubbery. Although in the twilight you can see no smoke, your nose picks up the familiar smell of smouldering leaves and garden waste. It would be sheer idiocy to cross the open lawn, so will you approach the house by creeping stealthily round the walls and beds to your left (turn to **308**) or to your right (turn to **350**)?

61

Your jabbing is ineffectual. You squirm and scrabble at the tussock, but it is no use. Your body, your head and, finally, your outstretched arms disappear beneath the surface of the water. Your adventure ends here.

62

You point your sword menacingly in the direction of the shape in the corner. Light from the rising moon glints softly on the blade and gives you courage. 'Who's there?' you call out softly, but a pathetic whimper is the only response. The unknown is always frightening and fear is beginning to chill your heart once more. Will you now change your mind and strike at the shape (turn to 179) or persist in a gentler approach (turn to 12)?

63

You double up as if in pain: you retch, grunt and grimace. The guards get the message: something is wrong with you. But do they believe you? *Test your Luck*. If you are Lucky, turn to 101. If you are Unlucky, the guards laugh scornfully at your feeble attempt to trick them; they make doubly sure your bonds are secure. Turn to 160.

64

The noise in the bar is deafening. All you can hear is snatches of nearby conversations. 'No, it was *you* who said that to *her*,' a young woman shrieks.

'Five shinies? You must be joking,' a sailor growls.

'. . . or my name's not Pen—' the man talking to the barman says.

'Did you hear the one about the Allansian and the . . . ?' someone else asks.

'Baron den Snau: he's the evil son of a lizard who . . .'

Will you try to find a place to sit (turn to **75**) or leave and look for another tavern (turn to **222**)?

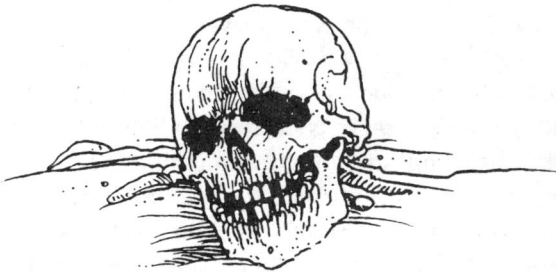

65

Test your Luck. If you are Lucky, the collapsing hut halves the remaining STAMINA of both your opponents (or of your remaining opponent, if only one is left); round odd numbers upwards when you halve their STAMINA scores. If you are Unlucky, the hut misses them altogether. Now return to **361** to finish the fight.

66

You pull out the medallion and dangle it in the air in front of Otus' eyes; this does the trick. He signals to Oman, and the steel-mesh net is drawn up by the pulley. You walk under it and are now faced by three enormous half-giants who are demanding to know your business. If you know a secret about two of them, add the number of the paragraph where you learned that secret to the number of this paragraph, then turn to the paragraph with that number. Otherwise, turn to **70**.

67

The magical descent comes to an end with you landing gently on the stone floor of a deep underground tunnel. You quickly take stock of the situation and see that there is only one way forward. As you take your first step, however, a hollow, horribly sinister laugh freezes you in your tracks. It seems to come from in front of you, but there is nothing to be seen. You hear a faint swishing sound and some sixth sense, honed from years of adventuring, makes you duck. This is just as well, because otherwise you would have been decapitated. 'Very good,' booms a deep voice, 'but remember: you have to be lucky every time, while I have to be lucky only once.' If you have a Potion of Invisibility, turn to **320**; otherwise, turn to **374**.

68

This will, of course, take you towards the source of the river's pollution. The stench in the afternoon sun is appalling. Short of swimming, which you definitely don't fancy, there is no way to cross the river here. Ahead of you, an unearthly grey cloud, streaked with gouts of livid green flame, appears between two hills: this is obviously the source of the pollution. Then you come across a series of platforms which resemble stepping-stones across the river, except that they are bobbing on the surface. Will you make for the grey-green cloud (turn to **169**), try to cross the river on the bobbing platforms (turn to **269**), or retrace your steps and head downstream (turn to **220**)?

69

You are walking through the land of the Flintskins, a primitive tribe which has survived for many centuries in these parts. A party of about twenty of these sturdy, pale-skinned hunters ambushes you. They are well armed with spears and bows. Will you fight (turn to **166**) or not (turn to **389**)?

70

You will have to fight all three half-giants at once! In each Attack Round, choose which opponent you are fighting; you win or lose as normal against him. Either of the other two can wound you if his Attack Strength is higher than yours in that round, but you cannot injure either of them until they become your chosen opponents – if you survive that long!

	SKILL	STAMINA
OPHIS	8	12
OMAN	8	10
OTUS	9	12

If by some miracle you win, and if you have a Truth-stone, you can use it on the dying Otus and demand to be told how to defeat Arachnos (turn to **298**). If you win, but you do not have a Truthstone, turn to **284**.

71

You are falling, floating magically down a hole which is lit by the phosphorescent glow of the rocks. Side tunnels lead off from the hole; will you take the side tunnel which you are approaching (turn to **372**) or will you wait (turn to **98**)?

72

In this fight, beware the Baron's sword, which is dipped in poison. He only has to nick you for the poison to enter your bloodstream. If you are wounded twice, you are dead. If you are wounded only once, you are strong enough to withstand the poison, but your Provisions will restore only 3 points to your STAMINA for the rest of this adventure.

BARON DEN SNAU   SKILL 7   STAMINA 12

If you defeat the Baron, turn to **119**.

73

You plunge deep into the bog. It becomes increasingly hard to walk: at every step you have to extract your foot with a squelch from thick mud. This is exhausting and by the time you reach the other side you have lost 2 STAMINA points. Turn to **24**.

74

It is easy for your opponent to see your swing and dodge it, and you leave yourself exposed. He thrusts the pointed end of his mace up into your chest and twists it savagely, to make sure that the blow is fatal. Your adventure is over.

75

You elbow your way through to the back of the room. Several faces in the crowd look vaguely familiar — fellow adventurers, no doubt, come to Arion on the same mission as yourself, and also trying to drown their disappointment in a flagon or two of ale. And there, sitting at a table with half a dozen empty flagons in front of him, is Fang-zen himself! Surrounded by cronies, he looks flushed with ale, success and his companions' toadying praise. Will you challenge him to a fight (turn to **5**) or try to join the group at his table (turn to **268**)?

76

After you have been trudging through the treacherous pools for ages, a strange sensation begins to creep over you: you feel impelled to turn in one particular direction. If you give in to this feeling, turn to **365**. Otherwise, turn to **195**.

77

You find yourself in a rather elegant high-ceilinged ballroom. Large, gold-framed portraits of the Baron's ancestors hang on the walls, but the pictures look

suspiciously new to you, and you decide that the
Baron's noble lineage may be pure invention. Apart
from a chandelier and some tables against the walls,
the room is bare. There are two sets of double doors
leading out of the ballroom. You extinguish the lamp
which the Ogre left in the room so that no light spills
out through the doors, but the lamp rattles noisily, so
you don't take it with you. A quick glance through
both sets of doorways confirms your guess that they
both lead to the main entrance-hall of the house. Will
you go through to the hall (turn to **197**) or climb back
outside and down the hatch (turn to **237**)?

78

The skeleton recounts a fascinating tale of dark deeds
and warns you to stay away from the ruined farmhouse. (Cross the Truthstone off your *Adventure Sheet*.)
You may now go northwards (turn to **263**) or turn
around and head south (turn to **355**).

79

You wipe your sword clean on the grass of the moor
and turn to walk away. With a roar the Cradoc rears
up behind you and scorches you with its breath (lose 2
STAMINA points). *Now* you remember: a Cradoc regen-
erates unless it is killed by having one of its heads
chopped off! But which head is it?

CRADOC   SKILL 7   STAMINA 8

If you win, with your final stroke will you chop off the
Dragon head (turn to **168**) or the Ogre head (turn to
147)?

80

The door swings shut behind you, blocking out the last remnant of the evening light from outside. Do you have a tinderbox? If you have, turn to **109**; if not, turn to **20**.

81

You wake up in the middle of a typical falling dream, in which you were leaning over a balcony, waving to someone, and then ... But if you're awake, why are you still falling? You land with a crash at the bottom of a small ravine over which you have sleep-walked. Deduct 4 points from your STAMINA. If you are still alive, you find that the mist has dispersed, but where are you? Turn to **379**.

82

You soon come to a junction, but the tunnel to the right leads directly back to the bottom of the magical tunnel you were recently floating down. You can see no point in returning there, so you carry straight on, down a dimly lit tunnel. Turn to **131**.

83

Cross 1 Gold Piece off your *Adventure Sheet*. The hag bites the coin to make sure it is genuine before scuttling off down a back alley. You wait for something to happen, but nothing does. You hurl the crumbling heather on to the ground in anger, and scratch at the bite one of the crone's countless lice has already given you. Turn to **388**.

84

Your bolt pierces Arachnos' black heart. His mocking laughter turns to a choked scream, and the dagger falls from his nerveless fingers. Telessa rushes into your arms. Without its leaders, Arachnos' army will soon turn to civil war. The land is safe . . . for now.

85

Only the ground and first floors of the building remain, and the first floor consists of just a landing, which is reached by stone stairs from the entrance hall where you are standing, plus a couple of rooms off it. The ruin is open to the sky and the marble floor of the entrance hall has partially collapsed. You can climb the stairs to the landing (turn to **138**) or leave the building after all (turn to **219**).

86

You bury your head under your forearms as best you can, but you still sustain 4 STAMINA points of injury to your head and shoulders. Turn to **199**.

That is exactly what Fang-zen was waiting for. He leaps up from his stool and lands the first blow on you while your back is turned (deduct 2 points from your STAMINA). You can count yourself lucky that he is rather drunk. Usually he is more or less your equal in a fight, but at the moment his SKILL is 3 less than whatever yours is, and his STAMINA is 10. If you win the fight, you have not killed him, merely hurt him badly. You wait for him to regain consciousness, then demand King Jonthane's letter from him. You point out that he's now in no fit condition to carry out the quest.

'That's what you think, scumbag,' Fang-zen snarls. 'And I haven't got the letter here. While we were fighting, a friend took it away and hid it. Too bad for you,' he sneers.

There's nothing you can do. You search him – and have to put up with his foul breath while you do so – but he's telling the truth. You leave the tavern, and now you either have to head west out of Arion (turn to **200**) or wander elsewhere in the city (turn to **222**).

88

A sturdy half-giant steps out from behind some boulders. 'I am Otus,' he says. 'You have something for me. I believe . . . A letter.' Once he has shown you a lock of the princess's golden hair, you hand over King Jonthane's letter of agreement. As the half-giant reads the letter, his face lights up with dark malice. 'Good,' he declares at last. 'My brothers and my master, Arachnos, will be pleased.' If you have heard the name Arachnos before, turn to **137**; otherwise, turn to **231**.

89

You succeed in tying the thread on to the needle in such a way that the needle is swinging free and horizontally. You rest the needle on the lodestone, where it sticks, then you wait a few minutes for the magic to transfer from the stone to the metal needle. You now have a crude compass. You don't know where you are, but you do know that you entered the marsh from the east and south. It makes sense, then, to assume that the further side of it may be reached by going to the west (turn to **34**) or to the north (turn to **361**).

90

'Him?' the guard says. 'Oh yes, we know him. And he regularly works for those two over there. You could have been a great help. Come to our station first thing tomorrow morning. You'll find me in room 56: take a note of the number. If your information has led to an arrest, there'll be something in it for you.' Will you now go to the Elfbane Bar across the road (turn to **189**) or call it a day (turn to **388**)?

91

You poke around in the burned-out house and, as the young man had said, find the body of a middle-aged woman. There is nothing else to be seen except piles of ash and badly burned beams. When you return to the other cottage, you find the door firmly barred against you. 'Go away!' the man yells through the door. 'You're not welcome here any more. Anyone interested in people dying is not for me.' You resent the injustice of it – you have paid the man, after all. You try to barge down the door but succeed only in bruising your shoulder. (Deduct 1 STAMINA point.) You have no choice now but to camp out in the open. Turn to **278**.

92

You wait until the Orc regains consciousness. If you have a Truthstone and want to use it on the Marsh Orc, turn to **205**; otherwise, it can tell you nothing. You leave it cringeing in the bog and continue on your way by turning to **55**, **154** or **365**.

93

You lose. The spurting blood is coming from a deep gash in your own hand. Deduct 2 STAMINA points and 6 Gold Pieces (that was your wager). If you want to play again, return to **132**. Otherwise you leave the tavern and may now either head west out of Arion (turn to **200**) or go elsewhere in the city (turn to **222**).

94

You pass another tunnel on the left with the same rank smell coming from it; it must be another entrance to the same system. Once again you ignore it and hurry straight ahead; turn to **2**.

95

The Truthstone can be used once and once only. It glows with an unearthly blue light which forces a creature with any intelligence (that is, not a plant or a rock, for instance) to tell the truth. Now turn to **357**.

96

Before you have travelled far, you encounter a Cradoc — and you soon wish you hadn't! These are two-headed monsters, one of whose heads is Dragon-like, while the other is Ogre-ish. You know that in the past you've heard rumours about some special thing they do, but you can't remember what it is — and anyway there is no time to think now, as the monster is charging at you, Dragon head breathing fire. It races towards you on all four legs, like a malformed lizard.

CRADOC   SKILL 8   STAMINA 10

If you win, turn to **79**.

97

Although it all happens too fast for your conscious mind, you somehow register the fact that the dark shape is Fang-zen and that he has hurled a spear at you. You fall to the ground, and the spear ricochets off a rock, snaps and falls harmlessly to the ground. Then Fang-zen himself is upon you, seeking revenge for the theft of his quest. He is a hardy adventurer too, and his SKILL is only 2 less than yours, while his STAMINA is 12. Only luck will see you through this fight unscathed. If you win, turn to **30**.

98

Another side tunnel is coming up. Will you take it (turn to **172**) or continue on down (turn to **210**)?

99

Ahead of you you hear a slurping noise which does not sound like the lapping of a rivulet of water. You creep ahead and see a brown, slippery-looking human-oid creature, kneeling on a tussock of grass and scooping up water with one hand. Will you attack it with your sword (turn to **118**) or jump on it and pin it to the ground (turn to **21**)? Or will you silently avoid it (turn to either **154** or **365**)?

100

You dash out through the front door and across the courtyard – only to find that the main gates are locked. You can't pretend to the Orc porter that nothing suspicious is going on: you will have to fight him before you can escape.

PORTER

SKILL 6   STAMINA 6

If you win, and if you bribed the porter to get into the Baron's grounds, you can take back however much you paid him before, plus 1 extra Gold Piece. You find a set of keys in the porter's gatehouse and use one to unlock the gates. Then you waste no further time before leaving the city and setting off westwards to try to find the kidnappers. Turn to **200**.

101

The guards notice what you are up to. They untie you from the pole and manhandle you in the direction of the elders' hut. If you want to try to escape at this point, turn to **112**; if you let them take you, turn to **352**.

102

It is difficult to know what to do. The village consists of only half a dozen peasant cottages, and there is no tavern or obvious place to stay. There is a burned-out shell of a cottage that looks uninhabited: if you spend the night there, you may at least avoid these surly villagers (turn to 224). Or you could knock on the door of any of the inhabited cottages – for instance, the one next door to the fire-damaged one (turn to 190).

103

Otus looks at the arrow in some puzzlement, then snaps it between two fingers and signals to Ophis. You turn to flee, but a crossbow bolt pierces your heart.

104

This is too much. Sensibly, you turn tail and flee. The tip of a green flame licks at your heels as you run, and your shoes immediately rot and fall off. If you have a spare pair of boots to wear, you put them on; if you do not, you must reduce your SKILL by one point for the rest of the adventure. You can now either try to cross the river by means of the bobbing platforms (turn to 269) or continue southwards past them (turn to 220).

105

If you have among your possessions either a moon symbol or a sun symbol or both, turn to 180; otherwise, turn to 46.

106

You enjoy a refreshing sleep which restores 2 lost STAMINA points. In the morning you find a piece of sharpened flint among the rocks, possibly evidence of a long-forgotten culture. A steep ravine rises a short distance away to the north, and you have come from the south, so will you now head east (turn to **399**) or west (turn to **4**)?

107

You fail to spot a tripwire, stretched at ankle height across the narrow path, and fall with a thud to the ground. Somewhere inside the house a bell starts to ring. You lie still, hardly daring to breathe. An Ogre comes to the end of the path and peers along it. It is rather gloomy here at this time of the evening, and you may be able to bluff him. Before advancing down the passage, he calls out, 'Who's there?' Will you say, 'It's only me' (turn to **7**), mew like a Scytheran Desert Cat (turn to **213**), or bark like a Kalagarian hound (turn to **327**)?

108

The Wraiths treat you to a particularly gruesome death. You have failed in your mission.

109

You strike a light and see that you are in a storeroom. Small, wooden packing-cases are stacked one on top of another in neat piles. Every case is stuffed with bits of paper – letters, receipts, invoices, and so on – and labelled with a date. It is now late in the second week of the ninth month, which is called Forests Golden in Khul. Will you search this month's file (turn to **174**) or last month's (turn to **312**)?

110

The Orc rains blows on your head with a large wooden spoon, but you shrug her off. You knock her unconscious and search the hut. You find a pot of stew simmering over an open fire. The combination of red-spotted toadstools and fish smells surprisingly good, and you quickly gulp down 2 STAMINA points' worth of sustenance. You also find 3 Gold Pieces and a medallion inscribed with the letter A which you may take if you wish. If you take the medallion, decide whether you wear it next to your skin or under your clothing, or you can stow it among your other possessions. If you want to have a look in another hut, turn to **6**. If you want to leave the village, you can go to the north (turn to **207**) or turn to the west (turn to **34**).

111

The rumblings are coming from Arachnos' forge. You veer off into the mouth of this tunnel, only to find that it slopes sharply downwards. You tumble down it and eventually end up in the forge. You execute a perfect roll, land on your feet, and face the truly enormous Ogre who is Arachnos' blacksmith. He seizes a newly tempered blade from a rack and lunges at you.

OGRE SMITH   SKILL 8   STAMINA 12

If you win, the dying Ogre falls backwards, upending a trough of molten metal. He dies in agony, and the red-hot liquid spills all over the floor, leaving you no choice but to leave by the forge door. You have time to snatch only a helmet, marked with the letter A, if you want to. In the passage outside, will you turn left (turn to **176**) or right (turn to **82**)?

112

Roll three dice. If the total is less than, or equal to, your current STAMINA score, turn to **191**; otherwise, turn to **129**.

113

A small fireball hurtles down the tunnel towards you! Will you use your backpack to protect yourself (turn to **282**) or not (turn to **86**)?

114

Roll two dice. If the total is less than, or equal to, your current SKILL, turn to **340**; if not, turn to **107**.

115

You swing by your fingertips from the last remaining stair, so as to reduce the distance you have to fall, then you let yourself go. If your current STAMINA score is under 12, you sprain your ankle on landing and must lose 1 SKILL point. Now you can leave the building; turn to **219**.

116

With an ear-splitting screech from its savage beak, the Pterolin attacks. The soulless glint of its eye is unnerving even to a hardened warrior like yourself.

MALE PTEROLIN   SKILL 7   STAMINA 8

You can escape down the tunnel at any time you like, but you must lose 2 STAMINA points as a talon rakes your back (turn to **208**). If you win, you can either go down the tunnel (turn to **208**) or climb back up the rope and continue westwards along the cliff (turn to **368**).

117

Assuming you have nothing better to do, will you go to the market-place (turn to **150**) or hang around the docks (turn to **171**)?

118

The creature wheels around in pain and surprise at your first strike, and you see that it is a Marsh Orc. It hurls a lump of mud at you, which allows it time to draw its sword.

MARSH ORC   SKILL 7   STAMINA 6

If you win, will you search the body (turn to **265**) or not? If you do not, turn to **154** or **365**.

119

The Baron lies dying on the floor, blood trickling from the corner of his mouth and bubbling with his final breaths. Will you now leave the house (turn to **100**) or question the Baron (turn to **244**)?

120

You crouch down and run into the hut. Luckily nobody spots you. Your eyes immediately smart and fill with tears. You can hear the Flintskin fumbling around, then you see his outline at the other end of the smoke-filled room. He picks up something from the floor and grunts in satisfaction. You knock him to the ground and grab whatever it is he went back for. Will you now try to barge through the mud wall at the back of the hut (turn to **194**) or leave by the proper entrance (turn to **376**)?

121

You kneel and peer into the crack. A few centimetres down is a small ledge, and the white object that caught your eye turns out to be the skeleton of a small animal – perhaps a hedgehog. Will you leave it alone and hurry on (turn to **146**) or poke around in the fissure (turn to **241**)?

122

Two of the fishermen look at each other. '*We* can't help you,' one of them says, 'but we know a man who can. You'd better visit Baron den Snau; he has a finger in every evil pie in north-east Khul, if you ask me.' They give you directions to the Baron's mansion. If you think it's worth visiting the Baron, turn to **273**; otherwise, you can visit the market-place, if you still need to (turn to **150**), or leave Arion and go in search of the kidnappers (turn to **200**).

123

You strip off your clothes, carefully laying them and the rest of your equipment close to the bars. You oil your whole body as much as the small quantity you have allows and, by means of considerable contortion (and at the cost of 1 STAMINA point), you squeeze between the bars. You find yourself on a narrow ledge between the bars and the drop, but it is wide enough for you to stand on to get dressed and equipped again. Then you finish your descent; turn to **67**.

124

You have no chance in combat against a menacing horde this size, but you may be able to offer them something, to see if you can pacify them. Will it be:

Money?	Turn to **362**
A medallion?	Turn to **338**
Pearls?	Turn to **255**
Your sword?	Turn to **36**
Food?	Turn to **301**

125

There is a wide courtyard between the gates and the front of the house. You notice a small gatehouse just inside the gates. It must be for a porter, so you rattle the wrought-iron gates and call out, 'Hello, is anyone there?' A suspiciously Orc-like porter sticks his head out of the gatehouse and snarls, 'Whaddya want?' You haven't finished explaining that you are a businessman who wants to see the Baron, when he interrupts by asking whether you have an appointment. Will you say yes (turn to **297**) or no (turn to **323**)?

126

The damp air on the fringes of the marsh has raised a plentiful crop of toadstools in the land you are now crossing. You feel tempted to try some. Will you sample some green-spotted toadstools (turn to **245**), some blue-spotted toadstools (turn to **136**) or some red-spotted toadstools (turn to **330**)? Or will you resist the temptation and press on (turn to **69**)?

127

Your eyes receive the full force of the acid and you are temporarily blinded. Reduce your Attack Strength by 5 points for this fight only.

SPIT VIPER   SKILL 4   STAMINA 4

If you win, you press on until you come to a place where the river is fordable. You can either wade across the river here (turn to **14**) or continue south (turn to **58**).

128

Alerted by the sounds of the struggle, the Dark Elf gardener creeps up behind you while you're rummaging among the Ogre's blood-soaked clothing and swings his scythe at you. A brilliant light flares in your head and then all is darkness – for ever.

129

You struggle, but the guards trip you up and pound your head on the ground for a while. Deduct 2 STAMINA points, then turn to **352**.

130

You race for the front door and slam it shut behind you. You can't go back in there: not even you can take on so many bats at once. You sprint across the courtyard for the main gates – but they are locked! If you bribed the porter to get in, turn to **280**; otherwise, turn to **251**.

131

You turn a corner to your left but, after only a few more metres, you find your way blocked by smooth rock. There is a straight crack down the centre of the rock, though, so you are sure this is some kind of door. You look around and find a lever set into the wall; it looks as if you can move it up (turn to **326**) or down (turn to **228**).

132

You both spread your non-fighting hands on the table and people at the table produce daggers for you. You place your bets and start to stab the point of the knife between your spread fingers. The game speeds up, but you keep pace with each other. The onlookers roar their approval as the silver blades begin to blur with speed. You are now so much into the rhythm of the game that you coolly dare to lift your eyes up from your hand and stare at Fang-zen. This unnerves him: he tries to meet your gaze but his eyes are constantly flicking back down to the table. All of a sudden, blood spurts! Roll two dice. If the total is less than, or equal to, your SKILL score, turn to **317**; if it is greater than your SKILL score, turn to **93**.

133

This is difficult. Roll four dice. If the total rolled is less than, or equal to, your current STAMINA score, you have enough strength to reach the end of the gulley before the boulder catches up with you and inflicts 6 STAMINA points of injury on you. If you survive, turn to **146**.

134

You pull the thread tight round what you reckon to be the centre of the needle and lift it off your thigh. But the needle slopes downwards and slips out of the knot; it sinks immediately out of sight into the brackish water of the bog. Turn to **290**.

135

The guard checks, but no one knows of anyone with that name, and there's no one resembling your vague description in the bar where you send the guards. You decide to turn in for the night; turn to **388**.

136

You suffer temporary paralysis. Roll one dice. If the number rolled is even, the paralysis affects your fighting arm and you must reduce your Attack Strength by 2 points for the duration of this fight. If it is odd, you suffer no major ill-effects. A Hoatzin has begun its soaring descent out of the sky towards you, with its wings folded under it so that the claws projecting from its wingtips are aimed straight at you. Its method of attack is to impale its victims with these claws, then tear at their flesh with its barbed beak.

HOATZIN   SKILL 6   STAMINA 6

If you win, you can taste some green-spotted toadstools (turn to **245**) or some red-spotted ones (turn to **330**), if you wish. Or you can push on (turn to **69**).

137

'You wait here now,' says Otus, jabbing a finger as thick as two ordinary fingers into your chest. 'I return with the princess in two days.' Will you do as he says (turn to **394**) or not (turn to **306**)?

138

It has been ages since the stairway experienced anything like your weight, and it begins to collapse. The steps, massive blocks of limestone, are wobbling under your feet as if you were in an earthquake. They're going . . . you're starting to fall. Will you jump for the next step up (turn to **358**) or down (turn to **293**)?

139

On closer inspection the jumble of rocks turns out to have some kind of order to it. In fact, the stones form a dolmen, a rough-and-ready tomb from ancient times. This would make an ideal place to spend the night, but first you have to clear out the Ghoul which has made this place its home ever since it sucked out the spirit of the dolmen's long-dead inhabitant.

GHOUL   SKILL 8   STAMINA 7

If, before the fight is over, you lose four Attack Rounds, turn to **53**. If you win, you settle down for the night but find that your lamp was broken during the fight. Cross it off your *Adventure Sheet* and turn to **106**.

140

You can deflect the green flame with a shield, but you will need to roll less than your current SKILL score with two dice three times. If you are successful all three times, turn to **13**; if you fail any roll, turn to **299**.

141

This time you are extra careful about tying the needle on to the thread in such a way that the needle is swinging free and horizontally. You rest the needle on the lodestone, where it sticks, and wait a few minutes for the magic to transfer from the stone to the metal needle. You now have a crude compass. You don't know where you are, but you believe that you entered the marsh from the east and south. It makes sense, then, to think that the further side of it may be reached by going westwards (turn to **34**) or northwards (turn to **361**).

142
The papers you snatched up are worthless, but you find a door and stumble through into the next room. Turn to **319**.

143
This seems a paltry sum to Ophis — not enough to turn him against Oman, but enough to turn him against you! Turn to **70**.

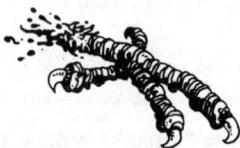

144
There is no shelter out here on the bleak moorland, so you can either push on through the night in an easterly (turn to **246**) or westerly (turn to **4**) direction, since there is a ravine a short way to the north, or you can return and investigate the hilltop (turn to **139**).

145
Riding on the crest of your current popularity in the tavern, you grab a handful of the landlord's jerkin, pull him halfway across the top of the bar and tell him in no uncertain terms what you think of his suggestion. You then leave the tavern; turn to **384**.

146

Three angry cavemen suddenly appear from among
the rocks. The terrain allows two of them to attack
you with their clubs at once. Choose which two are
involved in any Attack Round, then choose one of
these to fight. You win or lose as normal against
this one, while the other may wound you (if his
Attack Strength is higher) but you cannot wound
him.

	SKILL	STAMINA
First CAVEMAN	6	8
Second CAVEMAN	7	7
Third CAVEMAN	7	6

If you defeat all three cavemen, you leave the gulley
as quickly as possible, fearing another ambush. The
gulley has taken you down below the lip of the main
cliff. You scramble back up to the top and find an
impassable region of sharp, broken rocks and deep
fissures to the west. The only direction open to you
now is north. Turn to **382**.

147

Separated, the Ogre head lies on the ground, blood
oozing from its neck. You watch the Cradoc carefully, but is seems you have made the correct choice.
Slowly you back away from the monstrous corpse,
keeping your eyes fixed on it, until you are a safe
enough distance away to turn and run from the
horror. Eventually you allow yourself to slow to a
walk, but you no longer know where you are. Turn to
69.

148

You fumble around and cut your fighting hand on a piece of glass. Temporarily reduce your SKILL by 1 point until you have left Arion. Now leave the room by turning to **319**.

149

A female Marsh Orc pours scalding slops down on your head and shoulders; lose 2 STAMINA points. You tumble back to the ground. Return to **361** and finish the fight.

150

There are various articles you can buy from the stalls in the market and each costs 2 Gold Pieces. Choose as many as you like, but you would be advised not to spend all you have. Remember to deduct the appropriate amount of money from your *Adventure Sheet* as you accumulate items.

a large phial of sallow-seed oil
a needle and some thread
2 meals' worth of Provisions
a tinderbox and flint
a pair of old boots
an antique gilded arrow
a lodestone
two silver pearls
some rope
a throwing-knife
a fishing-net
a copper pendant

Once you have finished shopping, you can leave Arion to begin your quest (turn to **200**) or you can make your way down to the docks (turn to **171**).

151

You are struck by a fireball. Deduct 4 STAMINA points then turn to **215**.

152

It is not so much a question of whether you will succeed in this climb, but rather of how far up you will get before you fall. *Test your Luck*. If you are Lucky, turn to **182**; if you are Unlucky, turn to **44**.

153

The tunnel curves until it becomes clear that this is no more than a short crescent-shaped diversion from the main tunnel and that the two passages will soon join up again. The distinctive clicking sound of the tough plating of a Giant Millipede lets you know whose tunnel it is, however. Giant Millipedes are fiercely territorial beasts and resent any intrusion into their homes – except by edible creatures.

GIANT MILLIPEDE   SKILL 9   STAMINA 12

You can escape at any time (for the loss of 2 STAMINA points, as the Millipede nips your exposed back) by retreating and rejoining the main tunnel, but the Millipede will follow you. If you choose to escape, turn to 54. If you defeat the Millipede first and then advance to rejoin the main tunnel, turn to 275.

154

Struggling through the bewildering swamp, you find yourself in the middle of a patch of Tendril Grass. The clinging weeds trip you up and you fall, face down, into the bog. If you have been here before, turn to 226. If not, turn to 214.

155

The handle of the front door turns easily, and the door opens noiselessly on well-oiled hinges. Turn to 197.

156

You may now either search the farmhouse, if you

haven't already done so (turn to **391**), or carry on past it and head south (turn to **355**).

157

You land safely in the cold, oily water. It is so deep that your feet don't touch the bottom when you jump in. However, there are two problems. First, the water is cursed: if you drank water from a well earlier in your adventure (you will have WELL written on your *Adventure Sheet*), the poison it contained is now triggered and you must lose 6 STAMINA points. If you are still alive, you face the second problem: it is going to be very difficult to get out of here! The floor of the entrance hall is high above you and you can hear the sounds and then see the heads of Wraiths waiting for you up there. You swim around for a while but can find no obvious solution to your problem, except that there are enough fingerholds in the stonework for you to stand a chance of climbing up to the ground floor. Some of the Wraiths are now beginning to tumble into the water in their eagerness to reach you, but they can't swim and their bodies immediately decay on hitting the water. The stench is awful. Will you climb the wall in front of you (turn to **108**), behind you (turn to **167**), to your left (turn to **51**) or to your right (turn to **274**)?

158

Your hands grasp the window-ledge – and are lacerated by tiny slivers of glass which the Baron thoughtfully cemented there. You crash heavily to the ground; lose 2 STAMINA points. You can now make your way south towards the Baron's garden, to try to find a way into the house there (turn to **366**), or you can head north towards the front door of the house (turn to **114**).

159

The shadows are lengthening as you trudge up a ridge and look down on to another valley below. Will you camp until morning (turn to **277**) or press on through the night (turn to **246**)?

160

An hour or more passes. Then a message comes from the elders' hut for you to be brought before them. The guards untie you. Your hands are numb from the tight ropes, so you decide not to try to fight your way free just yet. Turn to **352**.

161

'Wrong again, Fang-zen,' you reply. 'It's just that I nearly died laughing at some tales of your attempts at wizardry. When that shape-change spell backfired and turned you into a Goblin . . . When are you going to get changed back again? I'd stick to thuggery if I were you, and leave the intellectual stuff to others!' His face darkens with rage and he starts to rise from his seat. 'Sit down, sit down,' you laugh. 'Can't you take a joke?' He settles back down, but there is a dangerous gleam in his eye. 'Now,' you continue, 'how about a game of pinfinger?' *Test your Luck*. If you are Lucky, turn to **132**. If you are Unlucky, Fang-zen refuses to play, and you get up to leave; turn to **87**.

162

Glantanka hears you. Her glorious rays burn away the mist and now you can see that you were not far from the edge of the marsh; you quickly make your way to dry ground. The ways of the gods are unclear to mortals, and you are desperate to get out of the marsh before Glantanka changes her mind. Turn to **281**.

163

You have scarcely started up the rock-face when a caveman appears out of one of the depressions above you and smashes a staff down on your knuckles. You fall directly into the path of the oncoming boulder. Your adventure ends here.

164

You decide to drip a few drops of the oil on to the hatch's rusty hinges, to prevent any unwelcome noises. Then you put the rest of the oil in its phial back in your pack, before opening the hatch and slipping through. Turn to **237**.

165

You penetrate a little way into the forest – far enough to be safely away from the open ground, but not too far, because in the twilight the deepest parts of the forest are frightening. And you are right to be frightened: had you gone any further, you would never have got out alive, for this forest hates intruders. You will get out eventually, but not before you have sustained 2 points of damage to your STAMINA as a result of being lashed by branches and brambles, tripped by roots and squeezed between tree-trunks. It is too late now to make for the village, so you will have to camp out in the open. Turn to **278**.

166

You mow down five or six of the advancing Flintskins before succumbing to a hail of blows. Your adventure is over.

167

When you have scrambled some way up the wall, the bit of it you are clinging to collapses — but inwards, not back towards the water. You land in a chute and slide, out of control, down and down. Then the chute ends . . . in thin air! You are sure that the moment of death has arrived for you. Turn to **71**.

168

Separated, the Dragon head lies on the ground, blood oozing from its neck. The Cradoc lies still, but you watch it intently, searching for the tiniest flicker of life. You watch it so intently, in fact, that you don't notice the Dragon head slithering across the grass towards you until it has fixed its jaws round your leg. In horror, you hack away at it, but it is too late. You collapse on to the ground, never to rise again.

169

The closer you get to the cloud, the more you can see that it has no obvious cause; it is not the outpouring from a smith's gigantic forge, for instance. It just seems to billow up from the earth, then drop back down on to the river and the ground. The whole place is barren and grey; leafless trees form stark silhouettes. But you have the distinct feeling that there is consciousness and intelligence behind this miasma, because the green flames have died down in exact proportion to your approach, as if they were waiting to see how close you would dare to come. And then, with a roar, the miasma attacks by shooting flame towards you. If you have a shield, turn to **140**. If you want to escape, turn to **104**. If you try to resist the miasma, turn to **299**.

170

You remember what a wizard once taught you: if you charge the needle with the magic of the lodestone and let it hang, parallel to the ground, from a piece of thread, the needle will point roughly north. 'Not exactly, mind you,' the gruff old wizard had said, 'just roughly.' He hadn't been able to explain why this worked but just put it down to earth magic. You hastily get the equipment together, then you sit down and rest the needle on your thigh while trying to tie the thread on to the middle of the needle. Roll two dice. If the total is less than, or equal to, your current SKILL score, turn to **89**; otherwise, turn to **134**.

171

The dockland area is a great place for gathering information. Boats put in here from all over Khul, and even from other continents. As an experienced sailor yourself, you have no difficulty in being accepted by a group of gnarled fishermen who are mending nets on one of the quays. You pass the time of day together discussing the weather before you turn to matters of wider interest. But the group is beginning to disperse: the tide is right for sailing. You can ask them if they know anything about Princess Telessa's kidnap (turn to **122**), where you can find some more scarlet pearls (turn to **364**), whether Fang-zen has left Arion yet (turn to **35**), or what they know about the gold-mining business (turn to **343**).

172

A short way along the tunnel you stumble across the fresh corpse of an Orc, no doubt the victim of some feud among Arachnos' troops. He has nothing worth taking, except a helmet engraved with Arachnos' 'A' symbol. You can put it on if you like, then turn to **210**.

173

In the back of the skiff the vague outline of a man appears. His sightless eyes gleam red as he says, 'What is your wish? Shall I take you to my master, or away from here?' Do you let him take you to his master, whoever that may be (turn to **247**), or away from here (turn to **367**)? Alternatively, you may not feel comfortable with this situation and decide to swim back to the tussock and return the way you came (turn to **29**).

174

You are flicking through bills and lists of freight the Baron has imported or exported so far this month, when the corner of a page ignites on the flame from your tinderbox. The flimsy pieces of paper and their dry, wooden boxes catch fire so quickly that is is almost like an explosion. Within seconds a fire is raging, out of control. You have time to grab one handful of paper and run out of the room: your hair is already starting to singe. Roll one dice. If you roll 6, turn to **261**; otherwise, turn to **192**.

175

If you have a shield, turn to **26**; otherwise, turn to **113**.

176

Before you have gone far, an Orc, busily looking over his shoulder, almost bumps into you. However, he recovers quickly and pulls out a vicious-looking sword.

ORC   SKILL 7   STAMINA 6

A rapid search of the body delivers 2 Gold Pieces into your hands. You carry on down the tunnel, but with increasing caution, as you soon begin to hear what sounds like a huge army massing. You round a corner and duck down behind a boulder in reaction to an astonishing sight. A huge cavern, whose roof is too far above you to be seen in the smoky distance, is filled with countless campfires, tents and all the baggage of an army. Thousands of Orcs, Goblins, Blackhearts, Dark Elves, Trolls and Ogres are milling around. Cruel officers lash their men to force them to work. From at least two places the screams of tortured men and animals arise. It is a vision of hell. There is certainly no way through here, and you must return the way you came. Turn to **131**.

177

The wall surrounding the Baron's house offers an unbroken barrier. There are no side doors. You can either return to the main gate, if you haven't already failed to get in that way (turn to **125**), or you can try to climb the wall (turn to **50**).

178

Do you have the A-medallion? If you do, turn to **262**; otherwise, turn to **39**.

179

In a single fluid movement, you turn and bring the blade of your sword scything down on to the unidentified shape, then you flee from the cottage before whatever it is can strike back. You run without looking back, terror in your heart, and camp for the night out in the open, with a good fire to keep your fear and any beasts at bay. Turn to **278**.

180

This causes considerable consternation. The elders murmur and talk among themselves for a long time. If you were brought here after trying to escape, turn to **46**; if you stayed tied to the post, turn to **322**.

181

The man is still alive when you reach him. 'It's you,' he gasps. 'King Jonthane sent me . . . new information . . . find . . . north of here . . .' He breathes his last. You leave his body for the crows: it is as clean a way to dispose of it as any other. You head north with your incomplete new information; turn to **289**.

182

When you do fall, by some miracle you land directly on top of your invisible opponent. This gives you time to get to your feet and fight him. Turn to **339**, but you may reduce his STAMINA by 1 point.

183

You walk halfway along the dank, gloomy passage. At the other end of it, in the garden, something large is stirring in the shrubbery. You decide to return to the front of the house. *Test your Luck*. If you are Lucky, turn to **340**; if you are Unlucky, turn to **107**.

184

Farigiss, the god of ice and cold, is puzzled by your appeal, but mortals so rarely call on him, except to curse him, that he is delighted to respond. He freezes the mist into a solid block of ice and you freeze to death inside it. Maybe in a few hundred or thousand years' time, you will be discovered, still preserved in the ice.

185

Test your Luck. If you are Lucky, you make it to the

top of the wall unharmed. If you are Unlucky, you fall awkwardly and twist your ankle (deduct 1 STAMINA point), then start again and complete your climb. There is a dank, narrow path between the wall and the house. You can jump for an upper window-ledge of the house (turn to **158**), or you can let yourself down into the passage, where you may go southwards towards the Baron's garden, to try to find a way into the house from there (turn to **366**), or you can head north towards the front door of the house (turn to **114**).

186

The slimy creature, which you now see is a Marsh Orc, tries to slip out from under you but fails. You have its head in a secure grip and you squeeze until the creature becomes unconscious. *Test your Luck*. If you are Lucky, turn to **265**; if you are Unlucky, turn to **92**.

187

Although it all happens too fast for your conscious mind, you somehow register the fact that the dark shape is Fang-zen and that he has hurled a spear at you. You fall to the ground; the spear ricochets off a rock – straight into your thigh. Deduct 2 points from your STAMINA. Then Fang-zen himself is upon you, seeking revenge for the theft of his quest. He is a hardy adventurer too, and his SKILL is only 2 less than yours, while his STAMINA is 12. Only luck will see you through this fight unscathed. If you win, turn to **30**.

188

You leap down from the rotting hull on to the spongy ground. You take out your compass and check your bearings. The contours of the lake's shoreline offer you the choices only of going east (turn to **207**) or north (turn to **346**).

189

A skein of geese in V-formation wings its way over-head as you turn into the bar – maybe this is a good omen. You sit on a high stool at the bar and try to engage the landlord in conversation, but he is too busy to do more than grunt. Mind you, your neighbour tells you that that's the most intelligent comment he's heard from the landlord in years. You swivel around on your stool to survey the scene. At that moment a vile-looking old crone walks into the bar, clutching some withered sprigs of heather. She is clearly a well-known figure, because she hardly has time to utter, 'Buy my lucky heather,' before the landlord has hustled her out through the door, prodding her with the brush end of a broom. Will you follow the horrid crone out into the street (turn to **10**) or investigate the gambling wheel at the back of the tavern (turn to **28**)?

190

You hammer on the door with the hilt of your sword, and eventually a surly young man answers it. He is prepared to put you up for a price: 1 Gold Piece and 4 meals' worth of Provisions, since the land here is rocky and unfruitful. Will you pay his price (turn to 313) or leave and go back to the burned-out cottage next door (turn to 224); or will you camp out in the open somewhere (turn to 278)?

191

You succeed in breaking out of their grip. You quickly knock one guard unconscious with a blow of your fist, then draw your sword to face the other, who is swinging a hatchet.

FLINTSKIN GUARD   SKILL 7   STAMINA 8

If the fight is still in progress after four Attack Rounds have been completed, more Flintskins are beginning to emerge from their huts (turn to 166). If you win before four rounds are over, turn to 238.

192

Before long the whole house will be ablaze. You can remain in the Baron's house for a maximum of *seven* further paragraphs. If by then you are not out in the courtyard, you will be roasted alive. Keep track on a piece of paper of how long you are taking to get out. The next location you turn to will be the first of the seven. The door back to the previous room is blocked by the fire. Will you examine the room you are in (turn to 148) or leave by the only available door (turn to 319)?

193

You quickly spot a trail of blood leading to a small hollow. One Troll-Orc is lying on the ground, dead or dying, and another is peering intently down on the wounded stranger. You begin to feel that the crows were *meant* to attract you here, to spring the trap. If you have a throwing-knife, turn to **363**; otherwise, you creep up behind the Troll-Orc (turn to **336**).

194

If your current STAMINA score is less than 12, in the time you spend trying to break through the wall you succumb to the smoke and flames, and your adventure is over. If your STAMINA score is currently 12 or over, you manage to break down the wall and escape through the village, which is now in a state of chaos. When you find time to investigate your trophy, you will see that it is a small branch of an ancient ebony tree, about thirty centimetres long, with a silver hexagram protruding slightly from one end. The branch also has the number 158 inscribed on it (make a note of this). It was evidently an important village totem. Now turn to **302**.

195

A short while later, a terrifying roar greets you from out of the mist ahead. Aeons ago, when this marsh was a lake, a terrible curse fell upon one stretch of shoreline and it became inhabited by Flesh-Eaters. These enormous serpentine monsters can slither over land or glide through water with astonishing speed. Only one now remains in Khul; it is old, as old as the hills, but its appetite is still strong and it makes a formidable opponent.

FLESH-EATER   SKILL 10   STAMINA 16

If you win, you can turn to either 311 or 154.

196

You waste no time in getting out of town. Turn to 69.

197

You are in the entrance-hall of the Baron's mansion. A wide staircase leads to the upper floors and there are doors off the hall to rooms on the ground floor. However, Baron den Snau himself has been alerted to your presence, and he is standing a little way up the staircase, looking down at you. 'What do you want, stranger?' he demands.

You reply curtly, 'Information.' Will you simultaneously rush at him up the stairs (turn to 395) or stand your ground (turn to 225)?

198

You pick a hut near the edge of the village and creep up to the doorway, which is covered by a piece of embroidered cloth. You cannot hear a sound from inside. Will you whisk the cloth aside and enter (turn to **250**) or leave the village (turn to **302**)?

199

There is no going back, so whatever the source of the fireball may have been, you are going to have to face it. You continue creeping down the tunnel on your belly. All of a sudden the tunnel ends at a small, underground cavern. On the floor of the cavern lies a pool of bubbling lava which occasionally emits fireballs at random intervals and in random directions. There are narrow ledges round both the left- and the right-hand walls of the cavern. You can take either one, but you will have to reach the tunnel opening on the other side of the cavern before you are overcome by the heat and the fumes. Roll one dice three times and make a note of the sequence of numbers you roll, as well as the total. If the total is between 3 and 9, turn to **22**; if it is between 10 and 18, turn to **252**.

200

Three days later, you are still walking towards the west. There has been no sign of the kidnappers, though occasionally you have felt yourself being watched. If you have King Jonthane's letter, the royal seal will show you where to go in order to meet the kidnappers. If you have come here without the letter, you have failed. Your action will cause the death of the beautiful and innocent princess, as King Jonthane warned you at the very start.

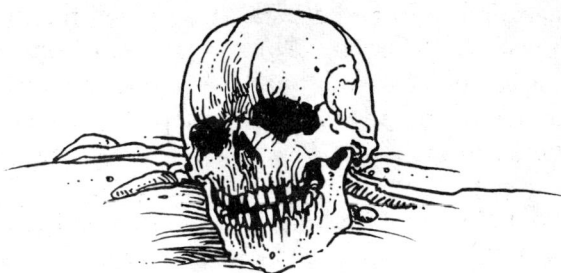

201

Few battles have come tougher than that. You feel elated at defeating the loathsome Pool Crawler; regain 1 LUCK point. You leap across the pool, using the belly-up corpse as a stepping-stone. The tunnel continues beyond the pool and ends at another door like the one through which you entered this tunnel. There is an identical lever in the wall. You check the ceiling, walls and floor but can see no obvious traps. Will you push the lever up (turn to 335) or pull it down (turn to 305)?

202

The porter greedily stuffs the money into his pouch and lets you in. (Deduct 4 Gold Pieces from your *Adventure Sheet*.) Then he disappears back inside the gatehouse. While the porter isn't looking, you can sneak along a pathway that skirts the west side of the house, if you like (turn to **183**), or you can boldly go up to the front door of the mansion (turn to **155**).

203

In the dark, you fall and pull a tendon in your thigh. Deduct 1 SKILL point and hobble on to **276**.

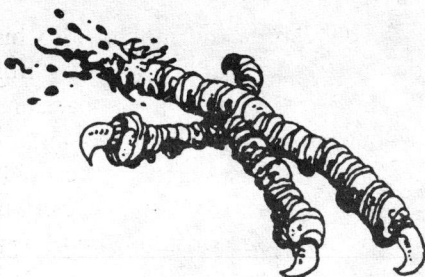

204

Nothing stirs as you enter the cottage. You glance quickly around then step across what remains of the single room to look out of the hole in the back wall which served as a window. A charred piece of sackcloth curtain flutters in the breeze. You shiver, although it is not cold: something evil has taken place here. Suddenly, out of the corner of your eye, you glimpse a faint movement from a rounded shape, tucked away in the corner of the room. In mounting fear, will you whirl and strike at the shape before it has a chance to do anything more (turn to **179**) or merely draw your sword in preparation for whatever it may turn out to be (turn to **62**)?

205

Cross the stone off your *Adventure Sheet*. The Orc rambles on for ages, but you learn little that could be called useful, except for a recipe for cooking red-spotted toadstools. You can continue on your way by turning to either **55**, **154** or **365**.

206

The pitchfork misses your ear by a hair's breadth and thuds, quivering, into a tree-trunk. Then the gardener is upon you, wielding a razor-sharp scythe.

GARDENER   SKILL 8   STAMINA 7

If you roll a double for your Attack Strength in any round, you have luckily cut through the wooden handle of the scythe, and you finish the Dark Elf off with ease. If the fight lasts longer than four rounds, turn to **291**. If you win sooner than that, turn to **366**.

207

You trudge on with a feeling of fear and hopelessness. Some marshes in Khul are home to rare creatures . . . and this one certainly is. Semerles are creatures frozen in time, relics from millions of years ago. Half-fish, half-reptiles, they are amphibious and store their meat underwater until it rots. A full-grown male Semerle – like the one facing you – can be two metres long and weigh up to a hundred kilos. Its squat body is solid muscle, and a flick of its tail can kill many creatures, if they survive its claws and the tusks protruding from its upper and lower jaws.

SEMERLE   SKILL 6   STAMINA 14

Every time you win an Attack Round, you must roll one dice to see if you manage to avoid its lashing tail. On a roll of 5–6, the tail strikes you and causes you 2 STAMINA points of injury. Of course, you don't have to make this roll after the Attack Round in which you kill the beast – if you get that far! If you survive, turn to **24**.

208

A short way down the tunnel you come across the sticky strands of a Giant Spider's web. Worse, you come across the spider itself! Its ability to see in the dark makes it more than a match for most people in tunnels like this.

GIANT SPIDER   SKILL 7   STAMINA 8

If you win, you slash through its web – and hear an ominous rumbling. You just have time to sprint forward to avoid a cave-in. There is no turning back now: the tunnel-mouth is blocked. Cross the rope off your *Adventure Sheet*, then turn to **18**.

209

The odds are too great, even for a great warrior like yourself. You fall to the ground, blood oozing from scores of wounds. Your adventure is over.

210

Faint rumblings are issuing from the mouth of the next side tunnel to appear. Will you enter this tunnel (turn to **111**) or continue descending (turn to **234**)?

211

The Bushel is a rather up-market establishment, where the bar-girls wear uniforms and the seats are covered in mock Lizardine leather. Entry is 2 Gold Pieces, but thereafter the food and drinks appear to be free. You can pay and go in (turn to **233**), go to the bar across the road instead (turn to **189**), or call it a day (turn to **388**).

212

This laziness is one of the magical effects the mist exerts upon you: you sink deeper and deeper into depression, as if the bog itself were sucking you down. But resolve still flickers in some corner of your mind, though it will take great mental strength to summon it up. Roll three dice. If the total is less than, or equal to, your current STAMINA score, turn to **236**; if it is greater, turn to **288**.

213

Desperation lends you an actor's skills. Even to you, your imitation of the rough tones of a Desert Cat are almost convincing. At any rate, the Ogre turns around and stomps off, cursing Tiddles under his breath. You make your way to the front of the house. Nothing stirs in the gatehouse on the far side of the wide courtyard as you turn the handle of the front door and it opens noiselessly on well-oiled hinges. Turn to **197**.

214

You come across the half-sunken, half-rotten shell of an ancient willow tree. Will you climb inside the hollow trunk (turn to **398**) or not (turn to **99**)?

215

If, with your *third* dice, you rolled 1–4, turn to **15**. If you rolled 5–6, turn to **324**.

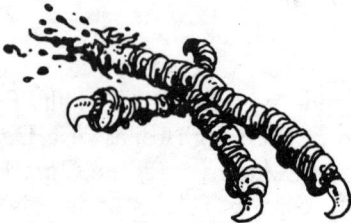

216

You make slow progress because you are spending time backtracking, looking for blades of crushed grass, overturned pebbles, broken twigs — anything that might show which way Otus went. By mid-morning you have progressed only a kilometre or two, and you stop to rest in the shade of a stand of oaks. You decide your best bet will be to enter dread Deathmoor and explore, since that is obviously where Otus was making for.

By noon of the following day you have reached the edge of Deathmoor. You are now confronted by a fast-flowing river whose surface is covered in scum and putrid fish. You need to find a way across the river: you can follow it upstream to the north (turn to **68**) or downstream to the south (turn to **220**).

217

Trapped between these two huge brutes, you stand no chance at all. Your adventure is over.

218

The papers you grabbed are worthless. You leave the blazing room by turning to **192**.

219

This a ghost town – literally! A crowd of Wraiths is coming down the street towards you, jostling one another for the first place and the chance of fresh meat. You decide that it will be wise to leave here. You can either go back inside the imposing building you have just left, and jump into the flooded basement, which is the only possible hiding-place (turn to **157**), or you can sprint down a side street and out of town (turn to **69**).

220

As you progress downstream, the river gets more and more sluggish, until you are almost keeping pace with the white underbellies of the dead fish in the river. You are walking along a narrow towpath with, on your left, tall gorse bushes that are armed with vicious thorns and, on your right, the oily river. And there, straight ahead of you, are two Blackhearts. These mutations – a cross between Dark Elves and Orcs – occasionally appear in northern Khul. The two facing you are on patrol and they have no hesitation in rushing forward to deal with you, swinging their jagged scimitars. Luckily for you, the path is so narrow that they can only get at you one at a time.

	SKILL	STAMINA
First BLACKHEART	7	10
Second BLACKHEART	6	8

Every time you lose an Attack Round, roll one extra dice. If you roll a 1, turn to **45**; if you roll a 6, turn to **259**; otherwise, continue with the fight. If you win, turn to **271**.

221

You will have to leap from one tussock to the next, so you carefully stow your precious compass away in your pouch first. In order to negotiate six tussocks, roll one dice six times. If the number rolled is ever the same as the number of the tussock you are jumping for (that is, if you roll 1 for the first jump, 2 for the second jump, and so on), you miss the tussock and fall into the water; turn to **387**. If you reach the sixth tussock unscathed, turn to **318**.

222

You turn into Creel-makers' Alley and see two more taverns further along, on opposite sides of the street. If you do not have the royal letter which the king and queen gave Fang-zen, you now feel that your task is hopeless and that you ought to start again, or perhaps go in search of another adventure. Otherwise, you may as well carry on drinking, now that you've started! Will you go to 'The Bushel' on the right (turn to **211**) or 'Elfbane Bar' on the left (turn to **189**?

223

You will have to fight the Troll-Orc.

TROLL-ORC   SKILL 7   STAMINA 8

If you win, turn to **27**.

224

As you approach the ruined cottage, you can smell that it has been burned down only recently. In fact, when your hand touches the doorpost, it is still slightly warm; inside, you can see smoke trickling from what were once roof-beams. But much worse is the fact that you also touched something sticky on the doorpost; even in the dim evening light you can see that it is blood. Will you cross the threshold of this cottage (turn to **204**) or beat a hasty retreat to the other place that caught your eye (turn to **190**)?

225

Like all bullies, the Baron is essentially a coward, caught up in a make-believe world in which he is brave. Since he believes his self-made myth, however, he advances down the stairs to fight you. Turn to **72**.

226

By now the monster under the water has been thoroughly aroused by all your coming and going. It ends your adventure with one chomp of its massive jaws.

227

There is still nothing in this room, even though you snatch one of the torches from the torture-chamber in order to have a good look. The voice is an Illusion Spell, triggered by opening the door between the two rooms. Return to **319**.

228

A hatch in the ceiling slides open and an Iron-eater drops on to your head. This jelly-like creature consumes anything made of iron in a matter of seconds. If you were wearing a helmet, you aren't any more! If you have a spare helmet, though, you may put it on. You shrug the creature to the floor, where you finish it off with a couple of slicing strokes from your sword. You now push the lever all the way up; turn to **326**.

229

As you cautiously lift one half of the double-doored hatch, the rusty hinges let out an awful creak. You wait a few moments, then a lamp flares in a downstairs window, bathing some of the garden in light. Will you run down the side passage (turn to **114**) or stay where you are (turn to **315**)?

230

You bend down as far as you can, you writhe, grimace and grunt as if in agony; in any language, this signifies severe pain. The guards approach to see what is up. You knee one of them on the chin and he collapses, unconscious, while you whip out your sword to fight the other.

FLINTSKIN GUARD   SKILL 7   STAMINA 8

If the fight is still in progress after four Attack Rounds have been completed, more Flintskins are beginning to emerge from their huts (turn to **166**). If you win before four rounds are over, turn to **238**.

231

It all starts to make sense now: Arachnos the Life-Stealer is up to his evil again. Centuries ago, in the far north-eastern promontory of Khul there stood a fair and prosperous trading city called Faleha; Arachnos gradually made himself master of all its revenue. Monetary gain was not his purpose, though he certainly needed to pay the increasing numbers of his servants, soldiers and minions. He is a creature of Chaos: he must sow Chaos and Evil wherever he goes and, unlike the usual thugs you come across in your adventures, he is intelligent enough to pursue more subtle plans for spreading Evil. In *that*, not wealth, lies his pleasure. Now it looks as though he has set his sights on Arion. He wants to manipulate the trade in gold until he controls enough of Arion to bring King Jonthane to his knees. No doubt his plans will not stop with controlling northern Khul; he intends to set up an Empire of Evil. Your thoughts are interrupted because Otus is still speaking to you. Turn to **137**.

232

You snatch the cylinder and jump back quickly in case anything happens. Nothing does, except that you broke off one of the skeleton's fingers when you took the cylinder. One end of the cylinder has a sun engraved on it, together with the number 55 (note this down). You stow the cylinder safely in your pouch. Will you now try on the crown (turn to **307**) or leave the ship (turn to **188**)?

233

Deduct 2 Gold Pieces from your *Adventure Sheet*, but restore up to 4 lost STAMINA points because of the food you eat in the Bushel. After eating, you take time to look around at the rest of the clientele. Raised voices attract your attention to a group at one of the tables. Guarded by a couple of henchmen who are at least half Troll, a couple of swarthy, well-to-do criminals have been treating their girlfriends to a night out, but it looks as though officers from the City Guard have tracked them down and are questioning them.

'You accuse me of arranging murder?' you hear one of the men shout. 'We are just honest plumbers – eh, Igiul?'

'Right, Oiram,' the other man agrees. 'We've been here all evening. There are plenty of witnesses – just look around.' Will you stay here, to be questioned by the guards (turn to **283**), or leave, knowing that as you've only just arrived in the bar you cannot help them. If you leave, you can either pop in to the bar across the road (turn to **189**) or call it a day (turn to **388**).

234

You can see the floor looming up below you, but there are more side tunnels still to come. You are beginning to enjoy the sensation of floating; will you take the next side tunnel (turn to **356**) or carry on down (turn to **9**)?

235

You are deeply asleep, but you suddenly wake up with a start. What was that? You can hear a snuffling sound to your left, and you leap up to confront a lone timber wolf which has been feasting on the Provisions from your backpack. Her eyes glint red in the firelight and her defence is savage, because back in her den her hungry cubs are anxiously awaiting her return.

TIMBER WOLF   SKILL 6   STAMINA 8

If you win, you find that she has eaten half your remaining Provisions (round odd numbers down). You doze fitfully for the rest of the night, and in the morning you try to pick up Otus' trail. Turn to **216**.

236

You force yourself to get up and carry on, reminding yourself of the old proverb that 'Where there's life, there's hope.' Your mind sparks into action again. If you have a lodestone *and* a needle *and* some thread, turn to **170**; otherwise, turn to **290**.

237

You drop lightly to the ground and find yourself, as expected, in a cellar. The floor is dusty and it doesn't look as though the room has been used for years. There are crates here and there, in no particular order, and half a bed, and a drawer from some long-forgotten chest. Will you search the room (turn to **3**) or not? If you decide not to, there is only a single exit: a wooden door to the east (turn to **80**).

238

You pause, hardly daring to believe that no one heard the fight, swift though it was, but nothing stirs. Will you now leave the village as quickly as possible (turn to 302) or prowl around (turn to 31)?

239

The pitchfork pins you to a tree by your sleeve – and by a chunk of flesh in your arm (lose 2 STAMINA points), so you are helpless. You grit your teeth and reach round to pull the pitchfork free with your other hand. Roll three dice. If the total is greater than your current STAMINA score, the Dark Elf reaches you before you have freed yourself, and the last thing you see is his scythe glinting in the dim light as it sweeps towards your throat. If the total is less than, or equal to, your current STAMINA score, you manage to free yourself in time to put up a fight.

GARDENER   SKILL 8   STAMINA 7

If at any time you roll a double for your Attack Strength, you have luckily cut through the wooden handle of the scythe, and you finish the Dark Elf off with ease. If the fight lasts longer than four rounds, turn to 291. If you win sooner than that, turn to 366.

240

His mace strikes you a glancing blow on the head. You manage to get to your feet, but you are groggy. Reduce your Attack Strength by one point for the duration of this fight only. Turn to 339.

241

You draw your sword and insert its tip into the fissure. This gulley is sacred to a tribe of primitive Cave People who propitiate the subterranean powers that caused the landslip with offerings of small animals. They have been watching your progress along the gulley and by poking your sword into the crack, you have insulted their gods. Behind you, they trundle a huge spherical boulder out of one of the caves and send it rolling down the slope towards you. The rumbling, crashing noise it makes as it gathers speed alerts you to your danger and you whirl around. Will you try to outrun the boulder (turn to **133**), look for a fissure wide enough or a cavern deep enough to hide in while the boulder thunders past (turn to **345**), scale one of the pock-marked rock-faces (turn to **163**) or try to leap over the oncoming boulder (turn to **249**)?

242

Do you have any sallow-seed oil? If you have, turn to **164**; otherwise, turn to **229**.

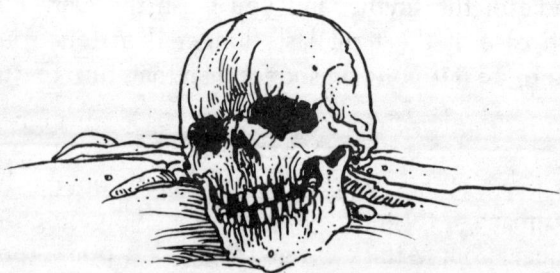

243

After a while, one of the guards mutters something to the other, then he gets up and goes off somewhere; by feigning severe stomach cramps, you trick the other guard into coming over. You knee him on the chin, at the same time chopping the side of your hand down hard on to the back of his neck. He crumples, unconscious, to the ground. Will you now escape from the village (turn to 302) or snatch up a flaming brand from the fire and toss it on to the thatched roof of the elders' hut (turn to 11)?

244

Do you have a Truthstone? If you do, and you wish to use it, turn to 264; otherwise, turn to 303.

245

You are immediately gripped by agonizing stomach cramps; lose 2 STAMINA points. You can now try some blue-spotted toadstools (turn to 136) or some red-spotted ones (turn to 330), if you wish, or you can hurry on (turn to 69).

246

You struggle on as best you can as deep night falls and the mists come down, but to no avail. Half-seen, half-recognized shapes loom, eerily glowing, out of the darkness, while fine moisture soaks you to the skin. The ghosts of Deathmoor lure you to your death over a cliff.

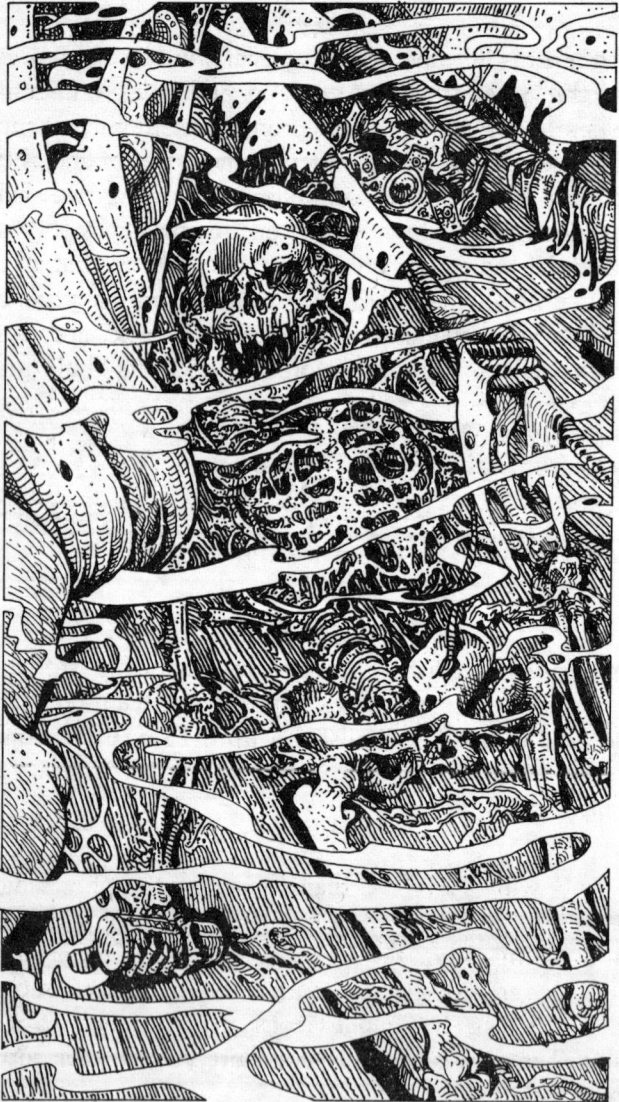

247

The skiff glides effortlessly over the lake without creating so much as a ripple on the water, until it comes to rest with a gentle bump against the rotting hull of an ancient longship. You climb out of the skiff and into the ship; the skiff floats away again. The ship has clearly been used for a royal burial: in the very middle of the ship lies an ancient skeleton and tattered rags of once-fine robes hang from its ribs, arms and legs. A jewelled crown has rolled off its head and is lying, a little way from it, on the deck. In one bony claw it clutches a metal cylinder. The ship is lying beached on the lake shore, so you can leave it without difficulty. Will you clamber ashore (turn to **188**), try on the crown (turn to **307**) or take the cylinder (turn to **232**)?

248

Ophis turns upon Oman in fury and, with cries of 'Thief!' begins to belabour him with his crossbow. Oman responds with his club. While they are thus distracted, you will have to get rid of Otus.

OTUS   SKILL 9   STAMINA 12

If you win, you find that Oman and Ophis have beaten each other senseless, and you are able to finish them off quickly. You turn back to the dying Otus and demand to be told how to defeat Arachnos. If you have a Truthstone, turn to **298**; otherwise, you can only watch him die and then turn to **284**.

249

Roll two dice. If the number rolled is less than, or equal to, your current SKILL score, you succeed in clearing the boulder, which hurtles harmlessly on, down the gulley, turn to **146**. Otherwise, you break your leg, and your adventure ends beneath the clubs of the cavemen.

250

The hut is deserted; perhaps it belongs to one of the elders who is in counsel at present. A rapid search of the hut reveals nothing. But by now the body of the Flintskin you killed earlier has been discovered, and the hunt is on for you. You have to sneak past six huts to reach comparative safety away from the village and the torch-bearing search-party. Roll one dice six times. If the number rolled is ever the same as the number of the hut you have reached, you've been discovered (turn to **41**). If you make it safely out of the village, turn to **302**.

251

You will have to fight the Orcish porter before you can get out.

PORTER   SKILL 6   STAMINA 6

If you win, you find a bunch of keys in his gatehouse and you waste no time in unlocking the gates and escaping back into the city. Turn to **359**.

252

If with your *second* dice you rolled 1–5, turn to **215**; if you rolled a 6, turn to **151**.

253

You are alone again in the marsh and still hopelessly lost. At times of crisis all intelligent creatures turn automatically to prayer: they send out a wordless appeal to powers mightier than themselves, and you are no exception. It seems that this is now your only hope. Will you pray to Arachnos (turn to **178**), Glantanka (turn to **332**) or Farigiss (turn to **184**)?

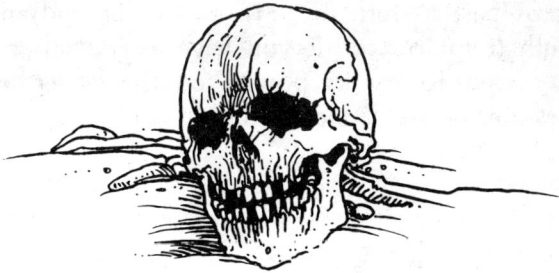

254

It's as well that you were careful, because in the deepening dusk you can only just make out the shape of the gardener, sitting with his back against a low bank. Unfortunately for you, however, his mother was a Dark Elf and so his hearing is exceptionally good. He has been listening to your approach for some minutes and hefting a pitchfork in anticipation. As soon as you are within range, he hurls the pitchfork in what he guesses to be your direction. *Test your Luck*. If you are Lucky turn to **206**; if you are Unlucky, turn to **239**.

255

The leading skeleton's jaw creaks open and shut a few times. It is trying to speak after years of silence. At last the words appear, but it takes such an effort that you find yourself mouthing them along with the Skeleton, as if willing it to get them out. 'What use have we of these, stranger?' the skeleton croaks. 'You are a fool, but you are not evil. You may go.' The skeletal horde stops pressing in on you and allows you to proceed on your way. You may now search the ruined farmhouse (turn to **391**), continue north-wards past it (turn to **263**), or turn around and go south (turn to **355**). If you have a Truthstone, you may wish to try its powers on the leader of the skeletons before you leave (turn to **78**).

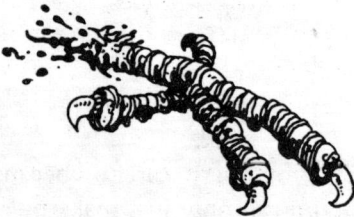

256

You succeed in sawing through the ropes that bind you, and the guards haven't noticed a thing! They are sitting on the ground to your left and right, a short distance in front of you. Will you try to sneak away from them (turn to **300**) or get them to approach you (turn to **230**), or will you wait (turn to **243**)?

257

The Baron is surprised by your attack. He was expecting you to spring a trap he has set into the second stair, but you leapt over it. So he hasn't even drawn his sword or tried to escape. Your charge ends with you head-butting him in the stomach. He doubles up in pain and jumps down to the foot of the stairs. You leap down after him, again luckily avoiding the trap, while he draws his sword. Turn to **72** to fight him, but first reduce his STAMINA by 1 point, since you have winded him.

258

You are trapped. When Arachnos' zoo-keeper comes round next, he will find a prize exhibit. Your adventure is over.

259

Shocked and in pain, you stumble into the gorse bushes. Deduct 1 extra STAMINA point before returning to **220** to continue the fight.

260

You kill the Troll-Orc outright and race down to the wounded human. Turn to **181**.

CODE

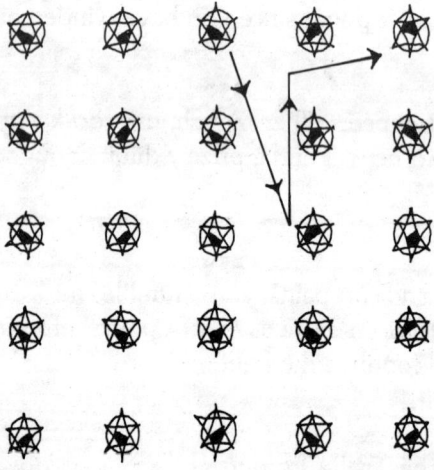

261

You shove the papers into your pouch. You have no time to examine them now, but in fact you have picked up a useful note. You can return to this location at any time to examine it: it appears to be the key to a code. For now, turn to **192** if you have started a fire; if you haven't, you leave and go into the next room by turning to **319**.

262

Arachnos the Life-Stealer heeds your call. He sucks your spirit from you, but not your moral awareness. Your torture for the rest of your days will be to commit horrid acts of evil as Arachnos' slave while still loathing yourself for doing so.

263

The slope going north beyond the farmhouse turns out to be steeper than it looked from a distance, and it is covered with loose stones and slate. You keep causing little avalanches on your way up and your hands are soon covered in scratches. At one point you slide several metres back down the slope and you are forced to pause, gathering your strength. Will you give up your attempt and go back down the slope (turn to **156**) or will you carry on (turn to **287**)?

264

You take out the Truthstone, and in its eerie light you see the cruelty of years etched on to the Baron's face as clearly as if you were reading a map or a book. Cross the Truthstone off your *Adventure Sheet* and turn to **303**.

265

You find 1 Gold Piece and a needle in the Orc's pockets. If you have recently lost a needle, turn to **141**. Otherwise, you carry on through the marsh by turning to **55**, **154** or **365**.

266

You reverse the Invisibility spell, just as the wise woman taught you. You find a curious object, whose purpose it is hard to guess at. It is about the size of a large key but it looks like a branding-iron, since it ends in a flat face. On the circular face is inscribed a crescent moon and the number '112'. Whatever it is, though, it feels important; restore 1 LUCK point. You store the object safely away in your backpack (add it to your possessions on your *Adventure Sheet*). You decide your best bet is to enter dread Deathmoor and explore, since it is obviously where Otus was heading.

By noon of the following day you have reached the edge of Deathmoor. You are faced with a fast-flowing river to cross; its surface is covered in scum and rotting fish. You need to find a way across the river: you can follow it upstream to the north (turn to **68**) or downstream to the south (turn to **220**).

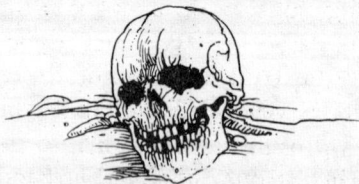

267

You find a silver whistle with an inscription in ancient Kabeshian, which you know well from your days at the Academy. The inscription reads 'Follow me', and you can also discern the number 333 (make a note of this). You blow into it and enjoy its clear, high note, but nothing else happens – except that you attract the attention of the Pterolin's mate. Like all the males of the species, this one is bigger and stronger than the female you have already met. Will you escape down the tunnel (turn to **208**) or stand and fight (turn to **116**)?

268

You lean over and whisper some extremely unpleasant threats into the ear of a small, weasel-faced man at Fang-zen's table, and he suddenly remembers an appointment elsewhere in town. Now that there's a stool available, you sit down. As soon as Fang-zen spots you, he begins to taunt you. 'Oh, it's you,' he sneers. 'Late as usual. The quest's mine, punk, and there's nothing you can do about it. What happened to make you late? Did you get doped by some Sleeping Grass, or did the milksop child of a weakling Sprite defeat you in a punch-up?' Will you respond to his taunts with insults of your own (turn to **161**) or get up and walk away (turn to **87**)?

There are four platforms with quite wide stretches of river in between them, but each platform is large enough for you to get a good run-up in order to jump for the next one. However, since each platform will sink into the foul water if you linger, you must simply run and jump four times non-stop. This makes the crossing progressively harder. Roll one dice four times. The first time, you are successful if you roll 1–5, for the second roll you need 1–4, for the third roll 1–3, and for the fourth and final roll 1–2. If you fall off the first platform, you can swim back to the eastern bank for the loss of 2 STAMINA points caused by damage from the poisonous water. If you fall off the second platform, you swim back to the eastern bank but lose 4 STAMINA points. If you fall off the third platform, you must swim on to the western bank and lose 4 STAMINA points. If you fall off the fourth platform, you swim to the western bank but lose 2 STAMINA points. If you end up on the western bank, as intended, turn to **159**. If you end up back on the eastern bank, you can either try again or give up and head south (turn to **220**) or investigate the bilious grey-green cloud (turn to **169**).

Tonight you rest in the comfort of bracken and heather (restore 2 STAMINA points), but Grinches get among your Provisions. Grinches are small, weasel-like creatures that are more of a nuisance than a danger. In the morning, you find that the sneaky creatures have spoiled 2 meals' worth of your Provisions before disappearing back into the undergrowth. You curse and carry on. About mid-morning of the next day, you come to the ruins of an ancient town. Will you bypass the town by heading east (turn to **69**) or walk along its eerily deserted main street (turn to **393**)?

You quickly search the bodies before tipping them into the river, where they immediately sink out of sight. On one of them, you find a medallion with an ornate 'A' on it, showing his allegiance to Arachnos. If you want to take the medallion, decide whether to wear it round your neck or beneath your clothing, or whether to stow it among your other possessions. On the other Blackheart you find a map which marks the

Blackhearts' encampment. The map does not make it clear whether there are any more – or even many more – Blackhearts back at the camp. If you want to risk a visit to the camp, turn to **386**. If you continue south, turn to **373**; if you would rather head north instead, turn to **68**.

272

You come to a stout wooden door on your left. You can hear a rumbling noise coming from behind it. Will you open it (turn to **348**) or press on (turn to **176**)?

273

You wait until evening before making your way to the Baron's mansion, as you figure that he's more likely to be in then; you also hope that the dark of night will enable you to move around more safely. The mansion is in the grand part of town where narrow alleys and busy streets and squares give way to leafy lanes and even the occasional field and copse. One such copse is unfortunately infested with Gutterlags: hyena-like scavengers which live in the suburbs but come down into the towns and cities at night to forage among the sewers for scraps of meat. Individually they prefer their meat cold and putrid, but a pack of Gutterlags, such as the one that is sneaking through the trees towards you, will attack live meat like yourself. You can fight the pack as if it were a single enemy because, once you have killed a few of them, the rest will scatter and slink back into the trees. But you cannot possibly defend yourself against all of them at once, and every even-numbered Attack Round you must reduce your STAMINA by 1 point, whatever else happens during that round.

GUTTERLAGS   SKILL 7   STAMINA 16

If you win, turn to **310**.

274

The Wraiths treat you to a particularly gruesome death.

275

After many twists and turns, the gloomy tunnel leads eventually to the lair of a Pool Crawler. This monster is the reason for the security doors you passed earlier in the tunnel. It lies, bubbling, in a pool of stagnant water, and Arachnos feeds it with the occasional Orc or Troll from his army. Two baleful eyes appear above the surface of the pool and size you up; the monster does not seem concerned with what it sees. It rears up out of its bed of mud and bones like an enormous toad. The warts on its mottled back hiss on contact with the air and give off a sickly-sweet odour. It whips out a long, spiny tongue towards you. If a Millipede is pursuing you, turn to **217**. Otherwise, you have to fight the monster.

POOL CRAWLER   SKILL 9   STAMINA 14

If you win, turn to **201**.

276

The mouth of the ravine through which you must go in order to escape is guarded by two Flintskin warriors. You will have to defeat them both to get through, but their posts are some distance from each other, so you can fight them one at a time.

	SKILL	STAMINA
First FLINTSKIN	7	8
Second FLINTSKIN	6	7

If you win, you are free. Turn to **16**.

277

During the evening the mists come down and you spend a chilly, restless night huddled under a low bank at the western foot of the ridge, before continuing on your way in the mid-morning, after the sun has broken through and dispersed the cloud. Will you go north (turn to **379**), south (turn to **355**) or west (turn to **8**)?

278

Although you plan to stay awake all night, the warmth from your campfire makes you drowsy and your head begins to nod forward on to your chest. Roll one dice. If you roll 1–3, turn to **235**; if you roll 4–6, turn to **371**.

279

Nothing is that simple. A monstrous alligator cuts through the water towards you. You dive under the water to attack its soft underbelly.

ALLIGATOR   SKILL 8   STAMINA 10

If you win, you haul yourself, panting, into the skiff. It is beautifully preserved, but in style and build it looks ancient. There are no oars, and there is no other way of moving the boat yourself. Then you see a slot which is evidently for money. If you have no money, or if you decide not to trust this alarming dinghy any longer, you can swim safely back to a tussock and return the way you came (turn to **29**). If you pay, will you put in 1 Gold Piece (turn to **247**) or 2 Gold Pieces (turn to **173**)?

280

'Quick,' you say, 'let me out.' The Orcish porter does not seem to be surprised: people often leave his master's presence in a hurry. He is deliberately, even insolently, slow in locating the key and unlocking the gates. But then you can escape back into the city. Turn to **359**.

281

You have reached the north-western edge of the marsh! Regain 2 LUCK points for surviving the mists and the marsh. If you had any tinder, you find that it is now too damp to use. You throw it away and gather more. As you forage, you allow the sunshine to warm you until your conscience pricks you to get a move on. Princess Telessa is waiting for you, and the fate of the whole world depends on you. You can regain 3 STAMINA points for your rest, but you have also picked up some leeches in the marsh. The number you roll on one dice is the number of leeches clinging to your flesh; it is also the number of STAMINA points you lose prising them off. You feel you are getting quite close to Arachnos' lair. Three ways forward look promising: you can go north-west (turn to **96**), north (turn to **270**) or north-east (turn to **126**).

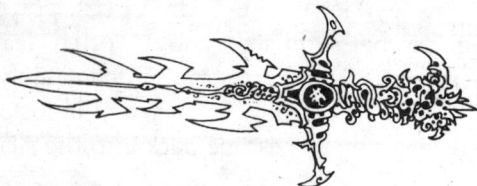

282

Although the heat of the fireball only scorches the stout leather, it destroys any of the following items you may have: arrow, thread, tinder and oil, and 1 meal's worth of Provisions. Turn to **199**.

283

'What's going on?' you ask the guard who has come to your table.

'There's been a murder on the other side of town,' the guard replies. 'A "business" rival of those two villains over there was conveniently trampled by a horse. No witnesses, and our only clue is a bit of torn handkerchief which the victim was clutching.'

A name pops into your mind; you think you might have overheard who the murderer may be. Will you say:

Anfold?	Turn to **369**
Twygarl?	Turn to **17**
Marinus?	Turn to **392**
Pengarl?	Turn to **90**
Elfbane?	Turn to **135**
Penfold?	Turn to **294**

284

You burst into Arachnos' chambers — and are faced with the most extraordinary sight of your life. The room is filled with mirrors; you estimate that there must be about four hundred of them. They are arranged so that they all show the same image: Arachnos, who is laughing at you and holding a dagger to Princess Telessa's neck. Which one, of all these images, is the original? You have grabbed Ophis' crossbow. Even though you can have only one shot, you are confident that you will be able to make it count: you can kill Arachnos without harming a hair on Telessa's head. But which image will you shoot at? If you don't know, you have to watch Arachnos kill Telessa, and you have failed.

285

You know that Pterolins are notorious for hoarding any trinkets they may find in the clothing of their victims. You locate the nest, secure the rope round a tree, and abseil down. The nest is on a ledge, but behind it a tunnel extends into the cliff. Will you rummage through the debris in and around the nest (turn to **267**) or investigate the tunnel first (turn to **208**)?

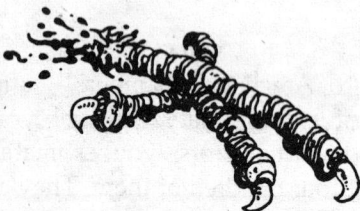

286

On your way up towards the Baron, you step on the second stair. This was a mistake, you realize, in the brief time it takes you to drop ten metres or so on to the spikes embedded in the ground below.

287

Your struggle up the slope costs you 1 STAMINA point in cuts and bruises. When you reach the top, you find that this is just the first in a series of ridges extending to the north like the bow-waves of a boat. You have committed yourself to an arduous journey. You must eat one meal from your Provisions here, just to keep your strength up, but it does not restore any STAMINA points.

On each of the next two days, as you struggle northwards and slightly to the west, following the contours of the land, you will have a hostile encounter. Roll one dice twice to find out from the list below what you must fight.

	SKILL	STAMINA
1. GARK	7	11
2. WILD BOAR	6	5
3. BRISTLE BEAST	5	7
4. HILL GIANT	9	11
5. HARRUN	6	7
6. GOBLIN	6	6

If you survive all the hazards of the Hopeless Hills, turn to **69**.

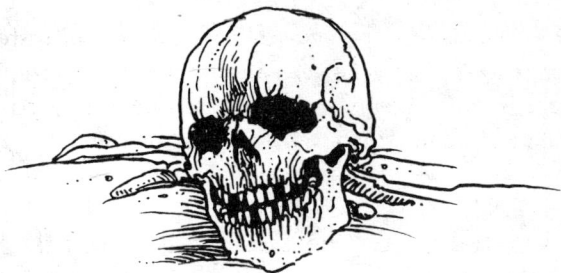

288

You see absolutely no reason to do anything. Life is horrible anyway, you reckon, so you might as well die here and now as somewhere else at a later date. And that is exactly what you do.

289

In the livid glow of a Deathmoor sunset, you come to an ancient door set in the hillside. Although it clearly originates in the lost civilization which once populated this land, you are certain that it is now the entrance to Arachnos' hide-out. You study in particular the three depressions in the door. If you have the three keys necessary to get in through the door, you can work out where to turn to next. Otherwise, you leave to look for another way in (turn to **246**).

290

You are completely and hopelessly lost. Only luck will see you through the marsh in these mists without a compass. As long as you are in this state, you will not be offered a choice of directions, since you have no means of knowing what direction you are going in. So now turn to either **55** or **154**.

291

A sleek, feline body leaps through the darkening air, claws slashing at your back. Your lifeblood is soon absorbed by the thirsty soil.

292

Unseen eyes are relieved to see you turn away from the gulley. But other eyes are also watching your progess — a Giant Nandibear is glad you chose to walk its way, since it is hungry. Larger and more ferocious than its smaller cousins, it rises on to its hind legs and lumbers at you, snarling. Even your heart sinks at the size of the beast.

GIANT NANDIBEAR   SKILL 9   STAMINA 14

If you survive four Attack Rounds, some cavemen suddenly pour out of the nearby gulley and begin to pelt the Nandibear with stones and crude wooden spears. The beast gives up the unequal struggle and trots away into the gathering twilight. You turn around to thank your rescuers, but they too have vanished. Puzzled, but grateful, you must continue on your way. Turn to **382**.

293
You fall and land awkwardly among the shattered blocks of stone on the floor below. Roll one dice: on an even number, you lose 2 STAMINA points: on an odd number, 3 STAMINA points. If you are still alive, you leave the building; turn to **219**.

294
The guard checks, but no one knows of anyone with that name, and there's no one resembling your vague description in the bar where you send the guards. You decide to turn in for the night; turn to **388**.

295

When you wake up, you are still walking. Although your mind recalls nothing, your muscles know that you have been sleep-walking for hours. You are lucky to be suffering nothing worse than exhaustion (deduct 2 STAMINA points). Still, at least the mist has dispersed now, but where are you? Turn to **379**.

296

The fight has taken place near one of the stilted huts of the village and you may have caused the hut to collapse during the fight. If the hut is still standing, you may turn to **385** to search it, if you wish. Alternatively, you can try to search another hut (turn to **6**) or leave the village altogether and continue north (turn to **207**) or turn west (turn to **34**).

297

That was stupid. If you do have to tell lies, you should at least make them less easy to see through. The Orcish porter glances at a diary and sees no entry under your name, whatever name you have given him. You may be able to bribe your way in, however, if you offer him 4 Gold Pieces (turn to **202**), or you can leave and look for another way in (turn to **177**).

298

Otus grits his teeth and tries to resist the mysterious power of the glowing Truthstone. He cannot quite resist, but he manages to give an enigmatic answer to your question, rather than the plain truth. His mind seems almost to be wandering, reviewing his life – as one is said to do at the moment of death. 'My parents died,' he croaks, 'after a sixth of my life; then for another twelfth I wandered the wastes until Arachnos found me – you could call that my coming of age, I suppose! For a seventh part I laboured in his mines, until he saw my potential and promoted me. I found a mate then, and five years later we had a child. He died, though, eight years ago, when he was half my age . . .' His voice trails off.

You cry out, 'But how old are you? Er . . . I mean, how old *were* you?' you add, as his eyes glaze over. Try to work out his age, then turn to **284**.

299

The flames do not burn you – they rot you, instantly! Roll one dice. If you roll 4–6, your flesh drops off your bones, and you are dead. If you roll 1–3, you must lose 6 STAMINA points before you can flee; if you are still alive, turn to **104**.

300

The guards spot you at once. They recapture you and give you a beating (deduct 3 STAMINA points) before dragging you off to the elders' hut. Turn to **352**.

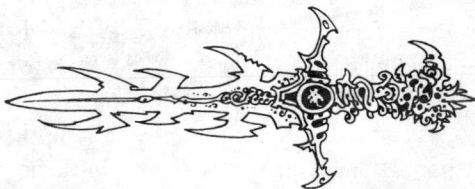

301

The leading skeleton's jaw creaks open and shut a few times; it is trying to speak, after years of silence. At last the words emerge, but it takes such an effort that you find yourself mouthing them along with the skeleton, as if willing it to get them out. 'What use have we of this, stranger?' the skeleton croaks. 'You are a fool, but you are not evil. You may go.' The skeletal horde stops pressing in on you and allows you to proceed on your way. You may now search the ruined farmhouse (turn to **391**), continue northwards past it (turn to **263**), or turn around and go south (turn to **355**). If you have a Truthstone, you may wish to try its powers on the leader of the Skeletons before you leave (turn to **78**).

302

Test your Luck. If you are Lucky, turn to **276**; if you are Unlucky, turn to **203**.

303

You kick the Baron's sword out of reach and bend over him. 'Quickly!' you hiss. 'What do you know about Princess Telessa's kidnap?'

'So that's what this is about,' the Baron gasps. 'Arachnos has her beneath Deathmoor. I made all the arrangements for him. Once he has Arion, King Jonthane . . . no choice . . .' The Baron is fading fast, but he rallies himself just enough to spit out the words: 'For this information you have killed me, but I'm glad to give it, since it will kill you. No one gets out of Deathmoor alive.' He struggles up to a half-sitting position and purses his lips. You step back, fearing he's going to spit at you, but instead he emits a shrill whistle. You hear a loud rustling sound and look up to see a dozen of the largest vampire bats you have ever seen boiling out of the roof towards you. Will you stand and fight (turn to **209**) or not (turn to **130**)?

304

Despite your host's vigil beside your bed, poker in hand, you sleep well and wake up, refreshed, in the morning. Regain 2 STAMINA points. In the morning you head west again, trying to pick up Otus' trail. Turn to **216**.

305

In the wall behind the lever lives a tiny Gering Snake. By pulling the lever down, you have allowed it to slither at lightning speed down the lever and sink its fangs into your finger. You will be dead within thirty seconds.

Stealthily, you follow Otus at a safe distance. Once, he half turns his head, as if sniffing the air, and you have to duck down behind a fallen tree-trunk, your heart in your mouth. After that, you let him get further ahead. It is clear that he is making for Deathmoor, a region of legendary harshness, into which no man within living memory has travelled and survived to tell the tale. Once, long ago, it was home to an advanced civilization, wise in the ways of the stars. Now it is a chill place of cruel, strange beasts and swirling, magical mists, the residue of the sorcerous battle which caused the downfall of that ancient culture. Folk say that when the mist descends, a traveller's sense of direction is utterly ruined, until only luck and common sense can bring one through. It will be very hard to track Otus through Deathmoor, but you are confident of your abilities. Suddenly a pheasant rises with a noisy clatter of wings from some tall grass to your left. Otus is too far ahead to hear it, but you wheel in that direction just in time to see a dark shape hurtle towards you. *Test your Luck*. If you are Lucky, turn to **97**; if you are Unlucky, turn to **187**.

307

You back away from the skeleton before trying the crown on, in case the action triggers it back to life or something . . . but the skeleton lies as still as ever and nothing untoward happens. After a while, you remove the crown and you feel some power impelling you to put it back on the skeleton's head, rather than take it with you. Outwardly you feel no different, but this selfless act means that your LUCK and SKILL are restored to their *Initial* levels. Will you now take the cylinder from the skeleton prince's hand (turn to **232**) or leave the ship (turn to **188**)?

308

As you creep through the shrubbery beside the west wall of the garden in the gathering dusk, some sixth sense tells you that something other than plant-life is in the patch of shrubs immediately ahead. Just then the Baron's pet, a tawny, sleek bundle of fur and savage claws, leaps with a low snarl out of the bushes and at your throat. You've never seen a Scytheran Desert Cat outside a zoo, and you certainly feel that that is where they belong – behind bars.

DESERT CAT   SKILL 8   STAMINA 10

If you win, you lie low for a while, making sure that the fight didn't attract any unwelcome attention, then you leave the cat's body to the slugs and continue on your way. A deeper shadow directly ahead of you shows you where there is a narrow passage running along the side of the house. You can take this passage towards the front of the house (turn to **114**) or stay at the back of the house (turn to **366**).

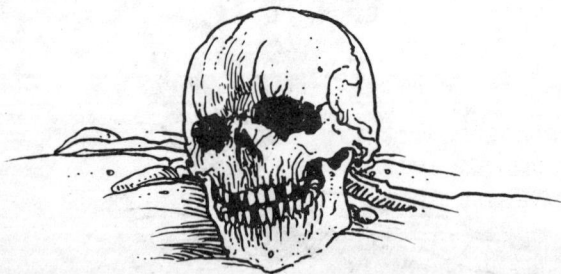

309

The badly wounded Troll-Orc on the ground has raised herself on to one elbow and with her last breath fired a poisoned dart from her blowpipe at you. Her aim is true: your adventure is over.

310

You are extra careful for the rest of your trek up to the Baron's house; the yellow sandstone of the mansion seems warm and welcoming in the glow of the late sun. The house is surrounded by a high wall. You can either pose as a businessman and approach the front gate boldly (turn to 125), or you can look for another way in (turn to 177).

311

A short while later, you find yourself in the middle of a particularly dense patch of mist. Parts of it seem to be swaying to and fro, like ghostly candle-flames flickering in a draught. This is unnerving, because you can feel no breezes to cause this motion. Then the Mere-folk talk to you in strange, half-whispering, half-whistling voices. 'Follow me,' they say, 'follow me.' You try to talk to them, but they do not understand. If you have a whistle which will let you talk to them, you will know where to turn to next. Otherwise, will you follow them (turn to 47) or not (turn to 253)?

312

You come across a very interesting letter. Written in black ink so thick that a blind person could trace the letters with his fingertips, it is signed with a spiky 'A'. It says that, of the three half-giants, the bearer of the letter (whose name is Otus) is more to be trusted than the other two, who loathe each other. Their love of money and their hostility towards each other make them, the letter continues, 'less loyal to me personally and less useful for our plan. So tell Otus alone the time and place of the Princess's picnic. He will do the rest.' Make a note of the hostility of the two half-giants, and of the number of this paragraph.

The Baron is clearly implicated in the kidnapping of Telessa. You are on the right trail: regain 1 LUCK point. At this moment, however, a spark leaps out of your tinderbox and the flimsy pieces of paper and their dry wooden boxes catch fire with a *whoomph!* Within seconds, the fire is raging out of control. You have time to grab one handful of paper and run: your eyebrows are already starting to singe. Roll one dice. If you roll a 6, turn to **261**; otherwise, turn to **218**.

313

Cross the items off your *Adventure Sheet*. You try to engage the man in conversation but he is not very forthcoming. All he says is: 'Don't you try to sweet-talk me. I'm an Outposter and proud of it. I know what you furriners are like – one of you killed Granny Longshanks next door. Huge feller, he were. So you just shut up and sleep on that bed there, and I'll watch you all night like a hawk. I've got food from you and that's all I want.' You wonder whether the 'huge feller' was the half-giant, Otus. Will you leave your surly host and investigate next door (turn to **91**) or stay where you are (turn to **304**)?

314

His mace strikes your shoulder, but not your fighting arm. Deduct 2 STAMINA points, then turn to **339** to fight the invisible warrior.

315

An Ogre sticks his head out of the window; he spots you standing like a frozen rabbit in the light, and tumbles out of the window. You get one strike in while he is in the course of doing this, but then he picks himself up and comes at you, wielding a double-headed axe.

OGRE   SKILL 7   STAMINA 8

If you win, will you stop to search the body (turn to **331**), scramble through the open window (turn to **77**), or go on through the hatch (turn to **237**)?

316

If you have either a throwing-knife or a piece of sharpened flint, turn to **37**; otherwise turn to **63**.

317

You win. The blood is spurting from a gash in Fang-zen's hand. You had wagered 6 Gold Pieces, but Fang-zen now confesses that he is broke. One of the few points of honour among thieves is never welshing on a bet; the others at the table scowl and sneer at Fang-zen, and start to draw clubs and knives. 'You had better give me the letter, then,' you say, and Fang-zen has no choice. He reluctantly pulls King Jonthane's letter out of his pouch and passes it across the table to you. The quest is now yours! You notice the royal seal, with its intertwined snakes looking like the number '88', before you tuck the letter safely away (add it to your *Adventure Sheet*) and turn to leave the tavern. *Test your Luck*. If you are Lucky, turn to **337**; if you are Unlucky, turn to **353**.

318

The sixth tussock is the last. As far as you can tell in the thick mist, only water now stretches ahead of you. What is more, a small skiff lies at rest, despite being apparently unanchored, a short way off to your right. Will you swim to the skiff (turn to **279**) or make your way back over the tussocks (turn to **29**)?

319

The room you now find yourself in is lit by torches in brackets on the walls. The flickering light reveals a grim torture-chamber. In the centre of the room stands a stretching-rack; on the walls, pincers, chisels and other sharp implements are neatly arrayed. You see whips with metal balls at the end of leather thongs, and a coffin-shaped box whose open lid reveals vicious spikes that are designed to sink slowly under the weight of the closed lid into the flesh of a victim lying in the coffin. As you step into the chamber, a plaintive voice from the room you have just left whimpers, 'Help! Help me, please!' Will you return to the previous room (turn to **227**) or leave the torture-chamber by the stone stairs leading up to a sound-proofed door (turn to **197**)?

320

You shrink back against the wall, pretending to be terrified, while you fumble in your pouch, saying, 'Mercy . . . mercy, lord. I have something for you.' Then you pull out the potion and down it at a single gulp (cross it off your *Adventure Sheet*). Immediately the invisible warrior becomes clear to you. He is no more than a renegade Dwarf, wielding a spiked and studded mace.

RENEGADE DWARF   SKILL 7   STAMINA 7

If you win, you find 4 Gold Pieces on his body. Turn to **59**.

321

You begin to see skeletons, complete or in fragments, littering the slopes on either side. Most of them are animal skeletons, but some are clearly human or human-oid. Wait! That one didn't move, did it? Surely, that hand didn't slide along the ground towards that wrist, then click into place? Will you make a run for the ruined farmhouse you can see ahead at the end of the valley (turn to **351**) or stand and face the rattling horde of human skeletons you now see gathering round you (turn to **124**)?

322

The Flintskins don't quite know what to make of you; they are not servants of Evil and they sense that you aren't either. Luckily for you, the opinion prevails among the elders that you must be on a mission against their arch-enemy, Arachnos. They solemnly present you with one of the tribe's most precious totems: it is a branch from an ancient ebony tree, about thirty centimetres long, with a silver hexagram protruding slightly from one end. The branch also has the number 158 inscribed on it (make a note of this). The Flintskins then escort you out of their safe gorge and see you on your way. Add 1 LUCK point, then turn to **16**.

323

'No,' you say, 'I have no appointment as such – but I do have these . . .' and you show him 2 Gold Pieces. A greedy glint comes into his eyes, and he furtively opens the gate just wide enough to let you in. (Deduct the gold from your *Adventure Sheet*.) He secretes the money somewhere about his foul person and disappears back inside the gatehouse while you make your way across the courtyard. When the porter isn't looking, you can sneak along a path that skirts the west side of the house, if you like (turn to **183**), or you can boldly go up to the front door of the mansion (turn to **155**).

324

The intoxicating fumes make you feel giddy and nauseous, and you reel about. *Test your Luck*. If you are Lucky, when you stagger you go in the direction of the cavern wall; if you are Unlucky, you fall into the pool of molten lava and perish horribly. If you are still alive, deduct 2 STAMINA points because of the effects of the fumes, then turn to **15**.

325

The door swings open to reveal an underground cave, which is lit by smoky torches in brackets on the walls.

You are confronted by two huge statues of reclining, horned, goat-like creatures. Beside each statue is the entrance to a passage. The statue on the left has a sign which reads:

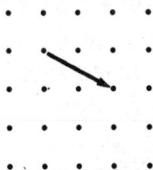

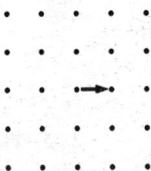

Will you take the passage to the left (turn to **383**) or to the right (turn to **71**)?

326

The door opens with a grinding noise and you step through into the gloom of the tunnel beyond. The door slams shut behind you so that you are now in pitch-blackness. If you have a tinderbox, flint and some oil, you can make a crude lamp; or you may have an actual lamp. Otherwise, you must reduce your SKILL by 1 point until you are told you are back in a well-lit area ... if you ever get there. Progressing mainly by your sense of touch, you come across a turning to the left; a rank smell is issuing from it. Will you take this turning (turn to **153**) or continue straight on (turn to **94**)?

327

'Dog?' says the Ogre with a puzzled look on his face. 'But the master don't have no dogs.' He then pulls a double-headed axe out of his belt and lumbers rapidly down the passage towards you. You barely have time to get to your feet and draw your sword. Turn to **397**.

328

Thinking quickly, you smash the phial of slippery oil on the ground in the Troll-Orc's path. He loses his footing and crashes heavily to the ground, where you dispatch him easily. Cross the oil off your *Adventure Sheet*, then turn to **181**.

329

As soon as you leave the bar, you are mugged by a team of professional footpads who had observed how much you won. They rob you of 2 meals' worth of Provisions and 8 Gold Pieces, before you scare them off with your sword. Make the appropriate adjustments to your *Adventure Sheet*, then turn to **388**.

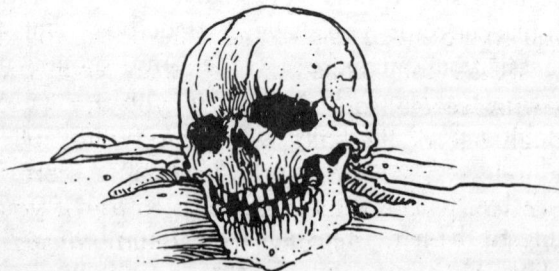

330

These toadstools are extremely nutritious: restore your STAMINA to its *Initial* level. Unfortunately, they are also very rare and you have already eaten all that are available in the vicinity. You can now try some green-spotted toadstools (turn to **245**) or some blue-spotted ones (turn to **136**), if you wish. Or you can continue on your way (turn to **69**).

331

Have you already dealt with the gardener? If you have, turn to **32**; otherwise, turn to **128**.

332

If your current LUCK score is 6 or above, turn to **162**. If it is less, nothing happens; return to **253** and try again.

333

You blow on the whistle to signal your agreement to the idea of following them. They lead you safely out of the north-western reaches of the marsh. Turn to **281**.

334

If you try to barge one of the stilts down, roll three dice; if the total rolled is less than your current STAMINA score, you succeed. If you try to hack through one of the stilts with your sword, roll two dice and get less than your current SKILL score. You decide which one of these methods to use. If you are successful, turn to **65**; otherwise, return to **361** and finish the fight.

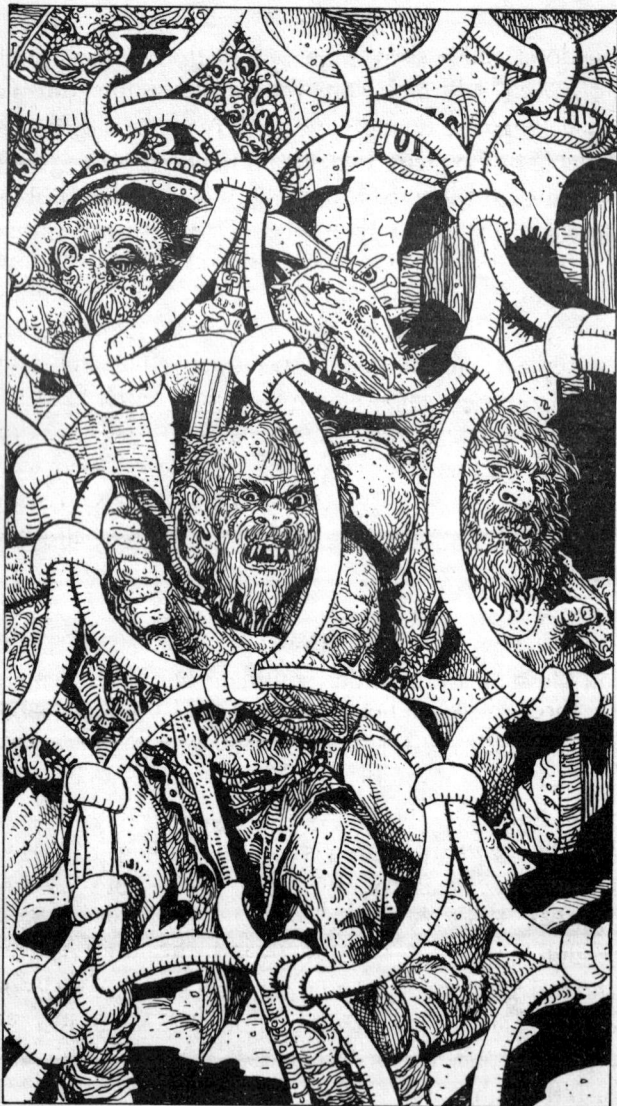

335

The door glides silently open and you step through into a well-lit tunnel. You walk on, but soon from up ahead you can hear the din of a large number of soldiers, and you see a glow coming from the huge cavern in which they are encamped. When a turning appears to your left, therefore, you decide to take it. You now find yourself in a short corridor which ends at a grandiose set of double doors. The sickening carvings on the doors, and the motif of the letter A interlaced, leave you in no doubt that this way leads to the chambers of Arachnos himself. However, there are three other doors in the corridor, with a signboard sticking out over each doorway. The signs read 'Ophis', 'Otus' and 'Oman'. You've already met Otus; the other two must be his half-giant brothers.

You can see all this through the mesh of a steel net which is attached by cords to bells on each of the three doors. There is no way to get through here except by attracting the attention of the three half-giants. You boldly jangle the bells and wait. In no time, the three half-giants come bustling out of their rooms. They are huge! Knotted muscles bulge on their arms and their chests seem about to break through their leather vests. One fingers an axe, another a crossbow, and the third a club studded with sharpened nails. It is Otus who peers at you through the mesh. Are you wearing an 'A'-helmet? If you are, turn to **396**; if you are not, turn to **19**.

336

You manage to wound the watching Troll-Orc, but then he spins around to defend himself against your surprise attack.

TROLL-ORC   SKILL 7   STAMINA 4

If the fight is not over by the end of the second Attack Round, turn to **309**. If you win, turn to **27**.

337

You shove your way through the crowd, who give way in awe at your exploits. Those who did not know you already are asking others your name. Restore 1 LUCK point. The barman catches your eye and beckons you over. Will you go and see what he wants (turn to **23**) or not (turn to **384**)?

338

The skeletons go berserk at the sight of the insignia of Arachnos, the dark lord who enslaved them and had them killed. They tear you to pieces. Once the crows and Mordidas have finished with you, your bones too will bleach on the hillside.

339

Because you cannot see your opponent, you must reduce your Attack Strength by 2 points for this fight, in addition to any SKILL penalties you may have already incurred. Only your lightning-swift reactions to the sounds of your enemy's breathing and his movements can save you now!

INVISIBLE WARRIOR   SKILL 7   STAMINA 7

If by chance you win, turn to **59**.

340

You sneak safely to the front of the house. No one stirs in the gatehouse at the far end of the courtyard as you turn the handle of the front door and it opens noiselessly on well-oiled hinges. Turn to **197**.

341

You let the bucket down then wind it back up, full of clear water. You dip your hand in and sip carefully. The water is refreshing and cool – and is a subtle poison, whose action may be triggered later in your adventure. Write WELL on your *Adventure Sheet*, then turn to **42**.

342

A pair of Marsh Ghosts loom out of the fog. The eyes of one glow a livid green, while the other's glow red. They use their magic to solidify their ghostly weapons, a silvery spear and a rune-inscribed sword, and they glide into the attack. If you have a shield, you can fight them one at a time. Otherwise, you must choose which one to fight as normal, while the other gets a free strike at you; you cannot wound it, but if its Attack Strength is higher than yours, it wounds you, causing the usual damage.

	SKILL	STAMINA
First MARSH GHOST	7	8
Second MARSH GHOST	7	8

If you win, you watch in astonishment as first their forms then their weapons dissolve into the mist. Turn to 214.

343

They all agree that they wish they had a piece of the action, since mining is much more profitable and secure than fishing. They cannot give you any specific information, however. You can go to the market-place, if you still need to (turn to 150), or you can now head west out of the city in search of the kidnappers (turn to 200).

344

You are about halfway down the slope when a savage Troll-Orc sprints out from cover and races down the hill towards you, a spear tucked under his arm, ready

to impale you. If you have some sallow-seed oil, turn
to **328**; otherwise, turn to **223**.

345
You race down the gulley ahead of the huge boulder,
but the time spent looking for somewhere to hide
allows the boulder to catch up with you; you must
lose 6 STAMINA points. If you survive, turn to **146**.

346
The marsh seems endless as you plod on for countless
hours, snatching a few hours of fitful sleep from time
to time, although the light never seems to change in
this eerie mist. You notice that, in avoiding the worst
areas of bog, you are gradually veering west. Will you
allow yourself to do this (turn to **281**) or will you
correct your course (turn to **73**)?

347

Only a few drops of the acid splash into your eyes. Reduce your Attack Strength by 2 points for this fight only.

SPIT VIPER   SKILL 4   STAMINA 4

If you win, you hurry on until you come to a place where the river is fordable. You can either wade across the river here (turn to **14**) or continue south (turn to **58**).

348

Steep steps on the other side of the door take you by surprise, and you stumble down them. You have entered Arachnos' forge, tended by a truly enormous Ogre, and your noisy entrance has attracted his attention. He seizes a newly tempered blade from a rack on the floor and lunges at you.

OGRE SMITH   SKILL 8   STAMINA 12

If you win, the dying Ogre falls back and upends a trough of molten metal. He dies in agony, and the red-hot liquid spills all over the floor, leaving you no choice but to leave by the forge door. You have time only to snatch a helmet, marked with the letter A, if you wish to. In the passage outside, will you turn left (turn to **176**) or right (turn to **82**)?

349

When a small fireball hurtles down the tunnel towards your face, you have no means of protection. You bury your face in your arms, but you must still lose 4 STAMINA points. Turn to **199**.

350

The smell of the bonfire increases; then you hear the sound of someone whistling tunelessly. Do you press forward with extra caution (turn to **254**) or retrace your steps and go round the other side of the garden (turn to **308**)?

351

If the total rolled is less than, or equal to, your current STAMINA score, you make it safely to the ruined farmhouse. If the total is greater than your STAMINA, the skeletons catch you out in the open and tear you to pieces in seconds. If you reach the farmhouse, you can at least defend yourself in the doorway as they come at you one by one. The skeletons have armed themselves with rusty tools that were lying around in the farmyard.

	SKILL	STAMINA
First SKELETON	6	5
Second SKELETON	6	4
Third SKELETON	6	4
Fourth SKELETON	6	5

Once you have defeated four skeletons, the remainder become strangely listless; their arms drop to their sides, their weapons clatter to the ground, and they crumple in piles of bones on the cobbled yard. Will you search the ruined farmhouse (turn to **391**), head north up the slope at the end of the valley (turn to **263**) or go back southwards (turn to **355**)?

352

You are taken into the elders' hut. The guards pin

your hands roughly behind your back and hold a dagger to your throat while your belongings are searched. If they find an A-medallion among your possessions, turn to **400**; otherwise, turn to **105**.

353

Your game of pinfinger with Fang-zen attracted the attention of most of the tavern's customers, including some decidedly unsavoury types, the kind of adventurer who would stab a defenceless Elf in the back with a poisoned blade. They saw Fang-zen give you the letter, and they rather want it for themselves. Two of them block your way out of the tavern. You will have to fight them both at once. Choose which one you will fight in any Attack Round, then roll dice as usual for the Attack Strengths of all three of you. You win or lose as normal against your chosen opponent. The other one will wound you if his Attack Strength is higher than yours, but he will miss if it is lower, while you can do nothing to hurt him in that round.

	SKILL	STAMINA
THUG	6	8
YOB	7	9

If you win, turn to **337**.

354

Your sword slices into something vital. Dark blood colours the water and you are free to pull yourself on to the tussock. Return to **221** to resume your perilous journey.

355

After a while, you come across a well; there is a bench beside it on which you are grateful to rest. Despite the well's obvious age, it looks clean and tidy, as if it has been properly maintained. A wooden bucket hangs from a chain. It is true that you are thirsty, and your flask also needs topping up. Will you drink from the well (turn to **341**) or not (turn to **42**)?

356

You walk down the tunnel – and suddenly you sink into the floor up to your knees. To your absolute horror, the 'floor' consists of thousands upon thousands of grey maggots, perfectly camouflaged in the colour of the surrounding rock. Now you have disturbed them into violent motion. Your thrashing carries you deeper into the mass of them. You trip and they fill your mouth with their disgusting wriggling. You cannot breathe . . .

357

You can now either go to the market-place (turn to **150**), or hang around the docks for a while (turn to **171**).

358

Test your Luck. If you are Lucky, turn to **375**; if you are Unlucky, turn to **293**.

359

As you make your way back down into the poorer districts of Arion, it all begins to make sense. Arachnos the Life-Stealer is up to his old evil ways again. Centuries ago, in the far north-eastern promontory of Khul there stood a fair and prosperous trading city called Faleha. Arachnos gradually made himself master of all its revenue. Monetary gain was not his purpose, though he certainly needed to pay the increasing numbers of his servants, soldiers and minions. Arachnos is a creature of Chaos. He must sow Chaos and Evil wherever he goes and, unlike the usual thugs you come across in your adventures, he is intelligent enough to pursue more subtle plans for spreading Evil. *That*, not wealth, is his pleasure. Now it looks as though he has set his sights on Arion. He wants to manipulate the trade in gold until he controls enough of Arion to bring King Jonthane to his knees. No doubt his plans will not stop at controlling just northern Khul; he plans to set up an Empire of Evil! There is no further time to waste. You resolve to be the one to put an end to his foul plans. You set off westwards, out of the city, to meet the kidnappers. Turn to **200**.

360

You get close enough to hear heated conversation going on inside – but, since you don't understand the language, this gets you nowhere. You estimate that there are maybe ten Flintskins inside. Will you leap through the doorway and attack (turn to **166**), go to one of the other huts (turn to **198**), grab a flaming branch from the bonfire and throw it on to the thatched roof of the elders' hut (turn to **11**) or sneak out of the village (turn to **302**)?

361

There is a breed of Orc that lives only in dank, gloomy places – by underground pools, or in marshes like this. They build small settlements of crude huts on stilts above the mud, and they eat raw fish and any other small creatures they can kill. In the thick mist you stumble into such a village before you know it. Luckily, most of the warriors are away on a hunting trip, but you still have to fight two Marsh Orcs at once. Choose which one to fight normally: you win or lose against this one as usual. Roll for the Attack Strength or the other Orc too: if it is higher than yours, he has wounded you, but you cannot injure him.

	SKILL	STAMINA
First MARSH ORC	7	8
Second MARSH ORC	7	7

As soon as you lose 4 or more STAMINA points during this fight, turn to **43**. If you win, turn to **296**.

362

The leading skeleton's jaw creaks open and shut a few times: it is trying to speak, after years of silence. At last the words emerge, but it takes such an effort that you find yourself mouthing them along with the skeleton, as if willing it to get them right. 'What use have we of this, stranger?' the skeleton croaks. 'You are a fool, but you are not evil. You may go.' The skeletal horde stops pressing in on you and allows you to proceed on your way. You may now search the ruined farmhouse (turn to **391**), continue northwards past it (turn to **263**), or turn around and go south (turn to **355**). If you have a Truthstone, you may wish to try its powers on the leader of the skeletons before you leave (turn to **78**).

363

Roll two dice. If the total is less than, or equal to, your current SKILL score, turn to **260**: otherwise, turn to **336**.

364

They look at one another in surprise. 'I thought everyone knew the Isles of Dawn are the place for them,' one of them says. Then they go off, laughing at the depth of your ignorance. You can now go to the market-place, if you still need to (turn to **150**), or you can head west out of the city in search of the kidnappers (turn to **200**).

365

The tussocks and streams, bogs and rushes, are starting to look terribly familiar. Could you be walking around in circles? If you have been here twice before, turn to **288**. Otherwise, turn to either **55**, **342**, or **76**.

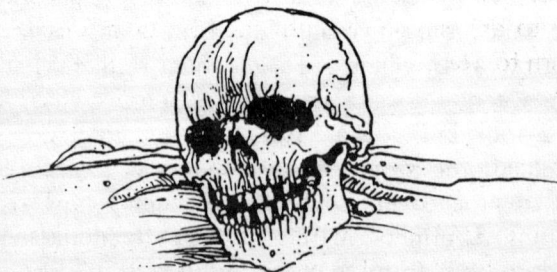

366

You reach the corner of the house and reconnoitre the whole expanse of the rear of the house. A smooth, well-trodden earth path runs along its length, bizarrely littered with the corpses of birds. You don't know what to make of this. The ground-floor windows are all securely locked, so there are only two ways to enter the house here: you could climb up some old, sturdy ivy and break in through an upper window (turn to 38), or you could lift a hatch-door which appears to lead to a cellar (turn to 242).

367

The helmsman takes you away from here all right. You float off into the mist, never to be seen again.

368

Keeping the cliff to your left, you continue westwards, following the movement of the sun overhead. The sun is dropping low over the horizon ahead of you when you come to a fork. The same landslip which caused the cliff to your left also formed a secondary gulley, running parallel to the cliff and sloping gently downwards. You can continue to the west along this gulley (turn to 25) or you can turn slightly to the north past it (turn to 292).

369

The guard checks, but no one knows of anyone with that name, and there's no one resembling your vague description in the bar where you send the guards. You decide to turn in for the night; turn to 388.

370

Otus pockets the object, but then makes a signal to Ophis. You turn to flee, but a crossbow pierces your heart.

371

You are only dozing lightly, so you can easily hear the approach of the ravenous timber wolf which has been attracted by the scent of your Provisions. Her eyes glint red in the firelight, and her defence is savage, because back in her den her hungry cubs are anxiously awaiting her return.

TIMBER WOLF   SKILL 6   STAMINA 8

If you win, you sleep fitfully for the rest of the night, and in the morning you try to pick up Otus' trail. Turn to 216.

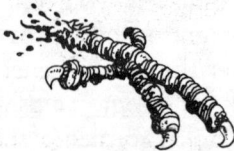

372

You land easily in the tunnel . . . and trigger a trap: a slab of rock crashes down in front of you, blocking the way ahead and releasing a swarm of hornets. You race out of the tunnel but have to lose 3 STAMINA points through their vicious stings. Moreover, the swarm pursues you for some distance down the hole, so you have to ignore the next side tunnel and turn to 210.

373

You have been following the river for a while when a slight movement in the bushes to your left attracts your attention and you turn your head towards it — which is precisely how Spit Vipers always get their victims. The large snake spits a ball of acid through the air at your eyes. *Test your Luck*. If you are Lucky, turn to **347**; if you are Unlucky, turn to **127**.

374

Will you charge down the passage, hoping to knock your invisible opponent off his feet (turn to **380**), swing your sword at him (turn to **74**) or try to climb back up the magical tunnel which brought you down (turn to **152**)?

375

Your fingers find a secure hold on the step above, as half a dozen huge blocks behind you crash all the way down into the basement. If your current STAMINA is 14 or more, turn to **49**; otherwise, turn to **293**.

376

You dash back out into the village square. You will be able to escape from the village, but first you will have to fight two Flintskins, one after the other, on your way out. Deduct 1 point from your Attack Strength for these fights only, because your eyes are still watering and smarting from the smoke.

	SKILL	STAMINA
First FLINTSKIN	6	6
Second FLINTSKIN	6	5

If you win, turn to **302**.

377

If you have a shield, turn to **26**; otherwise, turn to **349**.

378

You empty all your money on to the ground in front of the three half-giants; then you look at Ophis and say, 'Oman gave me this money, which he stole from you.' Ophis' face darkens in fury. If there are more than 10 Gold Pieces on the ground, turn to **248**; if there are 10 or fewer, turn to **143**.

379

You are walking through a valley; bleak hills rise to either side. You have a strong sense that you have been here before or maybe it's just that one piece of moorland looks much like another. The sun on your right is climbing in the sky, but it cannot dispel the fear in your heart as to what may lie ahead. Will you carry on (turn to **321**) or turn around (turn to **355**)?

380

He was not expecting this. You crash heavily into him, and you both fall to the floor. You pick yourself up, turn to where you now know him to be and prepare to fight. Turn to **339**.

381

As long as you have the shield, you will have to deduct STAMINA points only after every even-numbered Attack Round which you lose during any future fight. However, it may hamper you in some activities. Now turn to **357**.

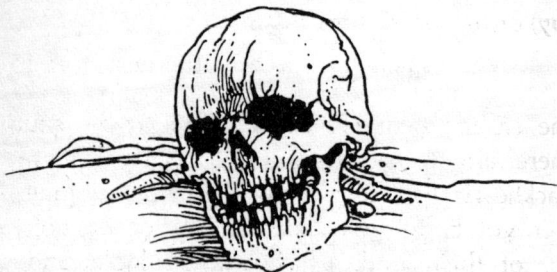

382

Regain 1 LUCK point for having survived Deathmoor so far. Night is drawing in as you approach a small hillock. There is something on top of the hillock: a pile of rocks, perhaps. You can either investigate it (turn to **139**) or ignore it (turn to **144**).

383

Spikes shoot out of the floor, walls and ceiling and impale you from all sides. Your death is mercifully swift.

384

Will you now head west out of the city, to begin your quest (turn to **200**), or stay in Arion for a while (turn to **222**)?

385

There is a ladder under the hut which goes up to a hole in the middle of the floor. As you are climbing the ladder, a female Orc pours scalding slops down on your head and shoulders! Lose 2 STAMINA points. You can continue up the ladder (turn to **110**) or go back down and try another hut (turn to **6**), or you may leave the village and continue to the north (turn to **207**) or turn west (turn to **34**).

386

The encampment lies a little way to the south-east. There are no guards, and it seems that the two Blackhearts you killed were based there alone. However, you find little of interest. You decide not to take any of their food, which to you looks and smells repulsive. You do notice a piece of broken stone with an 'S' on it, but you don't know what to make of that. You leave and return to the river-side, where you can now continue south (turn to **373**) or head north instead (turn to **68**).

387

Something slimy and very strong wraps itself round your ankle. You jab down at it with your sword, but it is pulling you under. *Test your Luck*. If you are Lucky, turn to **354**; if you are Unlucky, turn to **61**.

388

You return to your boat for the night. In the early hours of the morning, two fish-like shapes pull themselves over the side of your boat. Scarlet pearls are sacred to Pelagines, and they have sent a raiding-party to recover the one you 'stole' (as they see it) from Takio. Under their law, this crime is punishable by death. Pelagines are an amphibious race, equally at home on land or under water. Their fish-like heads belie cunning and intelligence, and the scales that cover their humanoid bodies are like armour plating. You can inflict only 1 STAMINA point of damage on them (unless you use LUCK too) in each Attack Round that you win. The male wields a trident, while the female advances tossing a coral-handled dagger from one hand to the other. In the narrow confines of your cabin, they have to approach one at a time.

	SKILL	STAMINA
PELAGINE	7	8
PELAGINETTE	6	5

If you win, you decide to stay awake for the rest of the night. In the morning, will you leave Arion to seek out Telessa's kidnappers (turn to **200**) or will you remain in the city for a while longer (turn to **117**)?

389

They approach cautiously, glancing warily at your sheathed sword. You think to yourself that there must come a time when the odds will be in your favour, so you let them blindfold you, truss you up and haul you off to their village, some kilometres away. This cluster of about thirty huts occupies the end of a ravine which is accessible only through a narrow pass and so is easy to defend. As soon as you enter the village, your blindfold is removed and you are surrounded by a crowd of curious women and children. They chatter away in a nasal language you have never heard before. The men drag you to a stout pole in the middle of the village square and tie you to it. Although you are still fully equipped, you are very securely tied up. As day gives way to night, a large bonfire is lit near you. People disperse to their evening meals, leaving only two men to stand guard over you, and you see the elders of the village go off into a large hut near by. Will you take this opportunity to try to escape (turn to 316) or will you wait (turn to 160)?

390

As you step forward to land your cowardly blow, one of Fang-zen's companions trips you up, while another stamps on your hand (deduct 1 SKILL point) and a third clubs you on the head (deduct 2 STAMINA points). When you regain consciousness, an entirely different group of people are seated at the table, and Fang-zen is nowhere to be seen. You stagger out of the tavern, reeking of the stale beer with which the floor was awash. You can now either head west out of Arion (turn to 200) or go to another tavern (turn to 222).

391

You have disturbed the horror which has made the ruins its home — and which is the cause of all the skeletons on the hillside. Once the chief servant of Arachnos, it grew too strong, so Arachnos posted it out here to guard the borders of his domain. But it has grown fat and lazy, and now it hates to have its rest disturbed. The Tantaflex uncoils its tentacles and oozes out of the basement towards where you are rummaging through a cupboard. A slight sucking noise alerts you, and you turn around to confront a creature out of your worst nightmares. Tentacles sprout from what should be its shoulders, and webbed feet squelch with mud from the basement pool. Piercing eyes glare at you from above a beak-like mouth. The tattered remnants of others' clothing cling to its body, and it is surrounded by the stench of its hoard of rotting flesh. By the time you turn from your looting, it has blocked the exits with its tentacles, so you will have to fight.

TANTAFLEX   SKILL 10   STAMINA 12

In the unlikely event that you win and gain your freedom out of the farmhouse, you can either head north up the slope at the end of the valley (turn to **263**) or turn back and make your way southwards (turn to **355**).

392
The guard checks, but no one knows of anyone with that name, and there's no one resembling your vague description in the bar where you send the guards. You decide to turn in for the night; turn to **388**.

393
You peer into empty windows as you walk along, but there is nothing of interest to be seen; even the

furniture has long ago rotted away to matchwood. Just dank stones remain, blackened by age and lichen, and streaked with dripping moisture. Some of the houses are still almost intact but the majority have completely collapsed. One semi-ruin was evidently once a building of some grandeur, perhaps the town hall. You duck inside, but it is as empty and gloomy as everywhere else. All the same, will you explore it (turn to **85**) or carry on down the street (turn to **219**)?

394
The first rule when dealing with creatures of Evil is *never* to trust them, not even for a moment. Frankly, it's astonishing that you have survived as many adventures as you claim. Otus will return with the princess all right — but she'll be in tiny pieces. You have failed in your quest.

395
Roll one dice. If you roll an even number, turn to **286**; if you roll an odd number, turn to **257**.

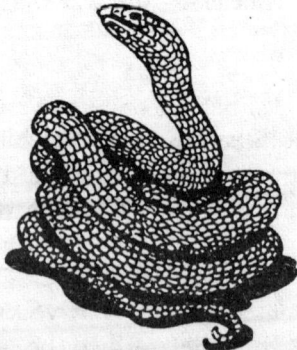

396

Otus fails to recognize you from your earlier meeting. He demands your pass. Will you present a moon symbol (turn to 370), an A-medallion (turn to 66) or an arrow (turn to 103)? If you have none of these, your deception is exposed and the giants refuse to let you through – in which case, your adventure is over.

397

Luckily for you, the narrow passage impedes the Ogre. He can only swing his axe overhead or prod at you with its spiked tip. So his SKILL score is less than it would otherwise have been.

OGRE   SKILL 7   STAMINA 10

If you win, you quickly search his body but find only 1 Gold Piece. The axe is too heavy for you to take. You return to the front of the mansion. No one is stirring in the gatehouse at the far side of the wide courtyard as you turn the handle of the front door and it opens noiselessly on well-oiled hinges. Turn to 197.

398

You find a perch halfway up the inside of the trunk where you can sit and be dry. You are exhausted, and you doze off. You dream of a time when the marsh was a vast inland sea, thriving with ships of trade, fair towns and joyful people. Restore 1 LUCK point and 2 STAMINA points. When you wake up, you can continue on your way by turning to either 154 or 99.

399

Before you have been travelling for more than an hour, the mists come down to surround you. They are so impenetrable that before long you are completely lost. Is that patch of mist thicker than the rest? You strain your eyes, but soon it dawns on you that you are faced by a Mist Demon, wielding a sceptre of adamantine ice.

MIST DEMON   SKILL 7   STAMINA 6

If you win, you blunder on, hopelessly lost, for hour after hour. Once you nearly fall over a cliff, and once you have to pull yourself back by your fingertips as you dangle over a crevasse. Eventually, however, the mist clears as suddenly as it appeared. Turn to 379.

400

The dagger held at your throat cuts deep. Your adventure ends here.